THE DARK RANGE

A big, rufous male coyote loped down a grassy slope and disappeared into a stand of oaks and digger pines.

THE DARK RANGE
A NATURALIST'S NIGHT NOTEBOOK

David Rains Wallace

illustrated by
Roger Bayless

A YOLLA BOLLY PRESS BOOK, PUBLISHED BY
Sierra Club Books
SAN FRANCISCO

Printed in the United States of America.

The Dark Range was developed and prepared for publication at
The Yolla Bolly Press, Covelo, California, under the supervision
of James and Carolyn Robertson during the fall and winter of 1977-78.
Production staff: Jay Stewart, Joyca Cunnan, Diana Fairbanks.

The Sierra Club, founded in 1892 by John Muir, has devoted
itself to the study and protection of the nation's scenic and
ecological resources—mountains, wetlands, woodlands,
wild shores, and rivers. All club publications are part of the
nonprofit effort the club carries on as a public trust.
There are some 50 chapters coast to coast, in Canada, Hawaii,
and Alaska. Participation is invited in the club's program
to enjoy and preserve wilderness everywhere.
Address: 530 Bush Street, San Francisco, California 94108.

Library of Congress Cataloguing in Publication Data

Wallace, David Rains, 1945-
The dark range.

Bibliography: p. 115.
Includes index.
1. Natural history—California—Yolla Bolly Mountains.
2. Nocturnal animals—California—Yolla Bolly Mountains.
I. Title.
QH105.C2W34   500.9'794'21   78-1452
ISBN 0-87156-212-X   ISBN 0-87156-251-0 pbk.

FIRST EDITION

*To my mother Sarah Wallace and
the memory of my father
S. Rains Wallace.*

Table of Contents

List of Illustrations

PAGE 84   *The marten zigzagged up the slope, tracing tangles of scent until he emerged onto a platform of bare rock interspersed with dwarfed lodgepole and foxtail pines.*

PAGE 93   *The cricket's antennae were agitated by a puff of displaced air as a flying squirrel glided in to land beside the woodpecker hole.*

PAGE 101   *The night was deceptively quiet until the lightning jumped the peaks; then it was cracked down the middle by a thick bolt of lightning.*

PAGE 106   *If I seem absent from the narrative, it's perhaps because I'm so omnipresent that the reader can't distinguish me from the background.*

Acknowledgments

A great many people helped to bring about this book. The English Department at Mills College provided working space by granting an assistantship to write the manuscript as an M.A. thesis. The Non-Game Section of the California Department of Fish and Game provided useful information on some of the animals I wrote about. The natural history staff of the Oakland Museum offered encouragement and constructive criticism at a time when both were needed. Arthur C. Smith of Hayward State University was a strong supporter of the manuscript and helped to straighten out some confusions about natural history. My wife Betsy was a reliable source of encouragement and sound advice from the beginning. Sierra Club Books and The Yolla Bolly Press provided the expertise and talent to turn the manuscript into a book beyond the dreams of a first-time author. My sincere thanks to all these, and to the many others who read and commented on the manuscript.

INTRODUCTION
The Wilderness of Night

Is not the midnight like central Africa to most?
Thoreau, *Journals*

FROM THE YOLLA BOLLY MOUNTAINS, the lights of the Sacramento Valley look like the luminescent patterns of some gigantic, deep ocean fish. A string of green lights—U.S. Interstate 5—runs down the middle of the valley. Delicate networks of white and orange radiate from it at intervals —the streetlights of towns such as Orland, Corning, and Red Bluff. To the north the string of lights expands into a glittering mass, as if the entire head of the fish glowed in the darkness. This is the city of Redding. There is little other indication of the sprawling valley civilization at night, even though the mountains are only a few dozen miles west of it. Distance quickly blurs the outlines of human structures. They fade into the imperfect geometry of organic form and appear prehistoric, as eternal or ephemeral as the earth itself.

The impression of temporal as well as spacial distance from civilization is enhanced by an optical illusion. The air in the valley is denser and dustier than the mountain air, so the lights blink and waver as though

1

the distant lamps were indeed underwater. This makes them seem cut off, unconcerned with the observer above them. By contrast, the stars shine steadily and brilliantly in the clear air of the mountains and seem close at hand. It is more than that; the mountain stars give an impression of attentiveness. They seem to be waiting—or listening.

The Yolla Bollys are part of one of the least visited national forest wilderness areas in California—the Yolla Bolly-Middle Eel Wilderness—and they are unusually quiet mountains. There are several reasons for this. The area is accessible only over many miles of dirt logging roads. Once reached, it is not very spectacular. The tallest peaks are a little over eight thousand feet and could be climbed barefoot with one hand tied. The scenery is not exceptional for the mountainous West. Most of the area is deep forest, so it is not a "realm of light" like the High Sierra. Water becomes scarce after June. There are a few small lakes and, of course, creeks and springs, but these are separated by wide dry spaces. The Yolla Bollys have been called desolate by some visitors.

This is not to say that the range—the southernmost part of the Klamath Mountains which cover most of northwest California—does not contain many pleasant things. There are alder-bordered cascades with native rainbow trout, meadows full of butterflies and wildflowers, stately forest groves. Several plants and a subspecies of meadow mouse are found nowhere else. There is a suggestion of history and folklore in the names of creeks and ridges—Opium Glade Ridge, Schoolmarm Creek, Frying Pan, Hole in the Ground—although the gold rush seems to have mostly bypassed the area. The name *Yolla Bolly* comes from the Wintun Indian terms for snow-covered, high peak. It loses something in translation.

If there is anything unusual about the Yolla Bollys, it is their quietude. Even today a visitor might wander for days in their inner reaches and meet no other person. The restless mind spins about for a few days and then begins to float more easily in the depths of the groves and the grassy glades. It is a good place to become aware of things that are usually ignored, particularly those things that are classified as nocturnal, and thereby often dismissed. It is a good place to confront modes of existence quite different from our own.

How is night different from day? It doesn't simply have less light than day; night has different light. Night is more than a negation. We can only speculate on the range of color and tonality perceived by eyes adapted to the light of moon and stars. Our aberrant diurnalism (most other mammals function at least as well at night as during the day) makes us see night as a biological underworld in which the more harried or nefarious organisms have taken refuge. This is true enough in populated areas where wild animals are persecuted. But there is really nothing subversive about night; it is an environmental factor to which a great many animals have adapted. Our own lack of adaptation is nothing to brag about.

The human fear of night is irrational and perhaps genetic. On a bus passing through the Klamath Mountains at night, a young man was overheard saying to his companion, "You sure wouldn't want to spend the night out there. You wouldn't last ten minutes with the things that are waiting for you out there." A lifetime resident of the area thought that there were still wolves in the wilderness, although zoologists have found no conclusive evidence that there were ever wolves in the California coastal mountains. Conversations with local people turn to stories of strange experiences in the nocturnal hills: an icy coldness floating in a sphere of colored light, an apelike figure beside a logging road, an unexplained cry, a sudden loud noise amid silence.

It is much easier to be skeptical about such stories under electric light than starlight. The lone observer beneath the Yolla Bolly stars may abruptly confront an abyss of credulity. A flashlight beam falls on blazing green eyes in the darkness, and the heart thumps, the spine tingles, the hair stands up. The deer or bear that coalesces around those fiery orbs

3

seems strangely unconcerned at the sudden dazzle of light. It manifests, at most, mild discomfort or curiosity. The flashlight wielder is slightly unnerved by this aplomb. He knows what *they* are and is still impressed. But what could *they* know about flashlights? They seem to disdain this sliver of light in their murky realm.

No technologist has yet published a scheme to end the unproductive hours of darkness. Perhaps it is too obvious that the darkness outside human vision is inextricably tangled with the darkness within. What, after all, is darker than the inside of a living human skull? Only death, injury, or surgery can let the light in. The mental terrain also has its night crawlers rustling the surface litter of the conscious mind. A light makes them pull back into their burrows so quickly that the observer retains only an impression of clandestine sliminess, unaware perhaps that they are fertilizing his imagination with their burrowings.

Human progress is often pictured as a movement from darkness to light. Perhaps it is time to discard the metaphor. There is nothing necessarily antithetical about darkness and intelligence. Whales and dolphins —considered among the more intelligent animals—spend their lives in the murk of the high seas. What cultures might a nocturnal intelligence create?

For humans there is no wilderness more difficult to explore than the night—not the seas, not the poles, not even the stars. What equipment can the explorer take along? The most powerful flashlight can only turn a small slice of night into day. Infrared scopes and special lenses are windows into the night, but windows imply walls. Darkness will not be remolded to human vision because it is a part of that vision. It is the vision that must be remolded. Dusk is a frontier that cannot be crossed on wheels.

The night described herein is a composite of many nights and therefore fictional. A true nocturne would devote ninety-nine pages to describing the qualities of silence and darkness and perhaps one page to events. Night is best explored by being quiet in the darkness; the longer the better. It may well be impossible for any single observer to do this long enough to learn anything substantive about darkness. Here is an undertaking large enough for the next thousand generations of humans. As we grub up the last metals and fuels, it begins to seem a more likely legacy than stars, seas, or poles. For the present, the night explorer can expect some rewards if no breakthroughs.

There are really three nights to explore in the Yolla Bollys. The mountains contain three altitudinal life zones with different climates and ecological arrangements. The lowest comprises the foothills and brush-covered ridges where the range rises out of the Sacramento Valley. In Merriam's somewhat old-fashioned classification, this is the Upper Sonoran zone. Many of its plants and animals range south into the desert state of Sonora in northwestern Mexico. Nights in this zone are hot and noisy. Next comes the Transition zone with cool, quiet nights. It consists for the most part of a pine and white fir forest, covering the canyons and ridges of the dissected plateau. Similar forests cover much of the mountainous West. Above the forest are the lakes, peaks, and meadows of the Canadian zone, where the nights are cold and mainly silent even in midsummer. Plants and animals similar to those that inhabit the Yolla Bolly peaks range north to the tundra. The Yolla Bolly-Middle Eel Wilderness does not encompass all of these three zones. The foothills are mostly outside the national forest, and the more accessible Transition zone areas have been thoroughly logged.

Despite, or perhaps because of, its heat and noisiness, the foothill night is not particularly intimidating. Sudden noises may startle a lone human, but uneasiness does not persist. The lively activity of the insects and other animals may be reassuring. The foothills are also the most tamed and occupied of the three zones. A more remote explanation for

5

this nocturnal amiability is the resemblance to the tropical savannah—our apparent cradle—without the large animals which can make the savannah a threatening place. In central California, where introduced Russian boars or feral pigs are present in the Sonoran zone, this situation changes. The pigs crash about, snort, and fix the observer with manlike eyes that glow blood red in a flashlight. They've filled the niche of the extirpated grizzly and appear to be increasing in range.

Night in the Transition zone is inspiring but rather disquieting. The tall, open forest soars toward the stars; moonbeams slant among the columnar trunks. There is a sense of gentle attentiveness, but it is dispassionate—a little frosty and resinous, like the night air. And there are gulches, canyons, thickets, and hidden glades where darkness is almost total, and sounds echo oddly or die too fast. The rush and chuckle of moving water is soothing when heard from beside a campfire, but if one lets the fire die down and listens more closely, the dark water may begin to say strange things.

As the terrain gets steeper and more rugged, the night becomes distinctly eerie. This feeling may have something to do with the predilection of gods for speaking from mountaintops. The openness of meadows and rock fields does not dilute darkness; it merely plays tricks with it. Blinding sheets of moonlight on grass or boulders render the surrounding shadows impenetrable. Winds keep the shadows moving, making a midnight walk on a high place unnerving if not dangerous. Even the stars can dazzle the eyes. In sheltered places, there is not so much a silence as a hush. Any break in the stillness, even a falling twig, comes as a shock.

The California mountains are perhaps most distinguished in the unusually varied and beautiful pine species they support. The Yolla Bollys are no exception. In each of the three life zones, the stars shine through the branches of a characteristic species of pine, a species endemic to California. In the foothills it is the digger pine—a slender, curved tree with sparse needles and bark thick enough to resist the heat. In the forest it is the straight sugar pine with purple bark and rich, deep green foliage. On the peaks it is the stout foxtail pine, crooked at the base from the weight of snow and dead at the top from the searing winds.

The brilliance of the light excited him. He screamed, dropped off his perch, and sailed over the canyon in a wide circle.

PART ONE
The Digger Pine

The Digger Pine

Listen to them, the children of the night.
. . . What music they make!
Bram Stoker, *Dracula*

THE YOLLA BOLLYS LOOK IMPRESSIVE ENOUGH when covered with snow in the winter, but it was July and they seemed distant and insignificant through the overheated air rising from the valley's baked soil. Patches of snow that remained on the bare summits were unconvincing viewed from a landscape in which the sun had shriveled almost everything except streamside vegetation and the sticky, night-flowering tarweeds in the brown grass. A few miles farther west, the foothills cut the peaks from view, first rising in gentle undulations, then breaking up into a maze of steep ravines with exposed stacks of red rock on ridgetops.

In the foothills the stately trees of the valley—blue, live, and valley oaks—spawned a race of dwarfs that swarmed out to cover all but the hottest, driest hillsides with a miniature park-woodland. The little trees had to drive their roots through a layer of lateritic orange clay to tap the ground water, and their leaves were adapted to letting very little of this hard-won moisture escape by transpiration. The blue oak's leaves had the texture of a suede boot, while those of the live oaks resembled plastic dishware.

11

This orange clay, termed hardpan by geologists, acts on the plants of the foothills (and by association the animals) like a giant flowerpot. During the winter, it filters rain into the earth so slowly that the ground stays wet most of that season. Herbs and grasses grow thickly then, but when the rains stop and the surface water dries up, everything except the oaks and tarweeds dries up too. Only in faults, gullies, and streambeds where the hardpan is cracked or worn away can a more varied vegetation grow. Most of the animal life of the hills retires into these places during the day.

Although the creek that runs through the hills had been dry for a month, the willows, cottonwoods, and laurels that lived on its underground flow made its bed bearable with their shade. Food shrubs such as toyon, poison oak, and wild grape grew on the bank; the sand was cool, and there were a few sinks of standing water. The air under the trees was soft and a little rank with decay, a process that had almost stopped in the harsh desiccation of the grassland.

In the open sunlight, the shrilling of cicadas was the only sound. In the creekbed, treehole mosquitoes with banded legs hung in the air or rested on leaves. A gray deer fly with an orange spot on its back buzzed past, followed by a jade green dragonfly. A steady, droning sound filled the shade, so numerous were the insects, and this had attracted birds. A wren hopped out of its hole on the bank and landed on an exposed tree root. Nuthatches probed the trunks, and phoebes and titmice fluttered among the leaves.

A yellow-striped garter snake swam across one of the sinks, driving tadpoles and minnows away beneath it. Then the snake had to change course to avoid a big predacious diving beetle. The pool was crowded with creatures that seemed faced with a thirsty death as the dry season proceeded. But most had a means of escape if the water dried up. The spidery striders on the surface could climb out and walk away at night;

the water boatmen and beetles could fly away; and the tadpoles would turn into air-breathing frogs and toads.

Outside the shade only turkey vultures and a few white butterflies moved. Those animals not in places like the creekbed had managed by various means to get under the clay, which luckily resists heat as well as water and tree roots. California ground squirrels rested in their nests several feet below the surface. Mice, beetles, scorpions, snakes, tarantulas, and salamanders found refuge in the cool darkness of these burrows. Whether strictly diurnal like the squirrels, or in varying degrees nocturnal or crepuscular, none could stand the full afternoon sun.

Even when the shadows began to stretch eastward, the heat didn't become more tolerable. It reached into some places that had been shady. Slanting sunlight passed under the foliage of the creekbed and struck the film of dust covering the surface of a pool. The striders seemed to move across a solid surface of sunlit dust. The light excited the flies and mosquitoes, and those that had been resting rose into the air. Violet green swallows appeared over the creekbed to catch insects above the trees. In a deserted pasture thousands of yellow star-thistles—alien weeds of overgrazed land—raised spiny flower heads that mimicked the sunburst descending toward the western ridge.

The Shadow Flood

In their burrows the ground squirrels sensed that the sun was getting low, and many came to the surface. They didn't have to; they had food in the burrows, but they were curious. One old squirrel, standing on his hind legs at the mouth of his burrow, saw a red-tailed hawk appear over the hilltop. He gave a long, whistling alarm call and ran into his hole. As the hawk's shadow slid across the colony, the squirrels (which were exactly the color of the dry grass) ran in all directions along the network of paths that connected the holes.

13

The hawk watched the commotion he had caused, but the squirrels needn't have panicked. He wasn't hunting; besides, the pasture had been claimed by a flock of western kingbirds. Although the gray and yellow kingbirds were somewhat smaller than robins, the hawk preferred to avoid them. At present they were inoffensively perching on posts or chasing insects across the meadow, but if they felt the hawk was encroaching, they would strenuously and persistently mob him. He kept flying up the creek.

The shadow of the western ridge advanced quickly across the pasture. Not long after the hawk passed, the sun slipped out of sight. It left no sunset, just a colorless patch in the sky as if even the blue had been burned away. There wasn't any moisture in the air to break the light into colors. A half moon that had been obscured by the sun's glare grew brighter in the southwest.

The hawk might have been flying over a land in flood. The creekbed and the gullies that ran into it were sunk in blue shadows, while the hilltops glowed with rosy light that grew brighter by contrast as the shadows deepened. In this light the life on the hilltops took on tropical brilliance. Skinks flicked their turquoise-striped tails over boulders of green serpentine. A pair of jade green dragonflies circled each other, collided, and fell together among the cadmium yellow flowers of some early-blossoming tarweeds. A quail covey burst out of a buckeye thicket from which the sun-scorched leaves were already falling and sailed into the shadows of the creekbed like a school of flying fish. The hawk saw it all in telescopic detail.

As he flew on, the slopes along the creek became steeper and higher. Patches of olive drab chaparral appeared on these steep slopes, and the feathery, gray green branches of digger pine reared above the oaks. The clay of the valley and foothills thinned out as mountain rocks began to thrust up, and the chaparral shrubs—chamise, manzanita, sticky monkey-flower, and yerba santa—were better adapted to the drained and exposed soil than were the oaks and grasses. The creekbed took a bend and ran into a canyon with bare walls the color of dried blood. There the foothills above merged into a single giant ridge, a tilted wall that stretched to the western horizon. Chaparral covered the ridge, but there were trees in the canyon. A blue pall over the valley was broken here and there by a flash of sunlight reflected from a window. The foothills were a patchwork of orange and violet.

The red-tailed hawk landed in a digger pine that curved over the edge of the canyon, shook out his feathers, and looked back the way he had come. He preened himself for a moment, but the brilliance of the light excited him. He screamed, dropped off his perch, and sailed over the canyon in a wide circle, still screaming. His cries intimidated the birds that had been calling and feeding in the chaparral. A brown, sickle-beaked California thrasher, cackling in a small live oak, stopped and ducked into the bushes. It absent-mindedly picked a green caterpillar off a leaf, wanting the hawk to go away.

Cricket Ghosts

The hawk landed back in the pine tree and looked around fiercely. But he found less and less to see as the shadows climbed the hillsides. He could still see the trees in the dimness of the canyon, of course, but the gloom didn't interest him. He needed bright light to see the distant movements of a squirrel in the grass or a rabbit in the bushes, bright light to see the differences in texture between fur and soil. As his excitement dissipated, he slouched on his perch and hung his head slightly. Two vultures flew over, and he cocked an eye at them until they were out of sight. Then he blinked and looked at nothing in particular. A few minutes later he dropped off the tree again and headed into the wilds of the canyon, toward his roost.

The birds began calling again as the hawk left the canyon, but since they also lived in the sunlit world that was being overtaken by shadows, their enthusiasm was waning. One bird, though, had just started to look around with interest. A great horned owl in a big laurel tree shifted in her perch and craned her neck up at the darkening sky. If the hawk's was a world of distance, the owl's was a world of depth, and the subtle contrasts of tone and color that excited her were beginning to appear on the canyon floor.

She watched a mouse move across a bed of fallen leaves that were a slightly different shade of brown than its body and saw a flash of the pale fur beneath the throat as it raised its head to sniff the air. But she didn't do anything. The scrub jays were still making inquisitive noises, and until they and the other birds were asleep, the owl would be patient. If they caught her out in the light, they would mob her, a more serious matter for her than for the hawk. Owls are sometimes killed by mobbing.

The bats were out—tiny western pipistrelles that seemed, as they fluttered around the canyon, more like big insects than mammals. They came out early because the small flying insects they ate—leafhoppers and gnats —were close to the ground then. Swallows that competed for the insects with them would occasionally swoop at the pipistrelles. Bats maneuver in the air better than birds, however, and they evaded the irate swallows easily. Later, as the clouds of insects rose higher in the night air, the larger bats would emerge. The little bats would have to be careful then; large bats are known to eat small ones.

Black-tailed deer appeared in the chaparral, all moving in the same uphill direction, probably toward water. Their graceful heraldic forms made a kind of tapestry among the shrubs. Below the canyon wall, a field cricket began to sing: "Treet. Treet. Treet." It was still very hot. Some trickles of cooler air ran over the sand of the creekbed, and a slight breeze stirred the trees, but the canyon remained parched and dusty. Rocks and soil that had been absorbing the sun's heat all day now radiated it back so what moisture there was in the air had nothing on which to condense. There would be no dew in the morning. Because of the heat and dryness, plants' leaf pores remained closed, holding back water vapor that might have lowered the temperature a little if released into the air. The dryness was cumulative.

The field cricket that had just started to sing was an ordinary-looking black cricket. But the insect sitting in a coffeeberry bush a few feet above him looked bizarre and might in fact have been the field cricket's ghost, if crickets had ghosts. He was the palest shade of green imaginable, his wings were transparent, and his legs and antennae seemed grotesquely overlong for his hunched-up body. When he lazily waved his antennae, the effect was distinctly ectoplasmic. He was a tree cricket; he and his kind are the main reason the foothills (and most other warm places) are noisy at night.

When the light in the canyon was just dim enough, the tree cricket raised his wings at right angles to his back and started to rub them together so fast that they faded into a blur. The sound it made was something between a police whistle and the ringing that comes after a blow to the skull. It was the field cricket's modest chirps drawn out to a banshee wail: "Treeeeeeeeeeeeeeeeeeeeeeeeeeeeeeee!"

The song stopped abruptly, as though the performer feared he had begun out of turn. There was a moment of silence, then a different tree cricket started up somewhere, and the first one began to sing, or stridulate, again. It is hard to locate a tree cricket from the noise he makes, because he sounds closer than he usually is. How he does this is not clear, but it must be helpful to him because the song is a warning to other male crickets to keep out of his breeding territory. The closer he sounds, the farther off his rivals can be expected to stay. Female crickets, who have ears in their front legs, are attracted by the singing and by a substance

Bats came out early, fluttering around the canyon. The graceful heraldic forms of black-tailed deer made a kind of tapestry among the shrubs.

secreted from between the males' wings as they stridulate. As a female drinks this, the male mates with her.

When it got a little darker, the banshee wail began to be punctuated by new stridulations, equally high-pitched but more rhythmic and syncopated. They sounded like: "Treee-eet . . . Treee-eeet . . . Treee-eet. . : ." A species of tree cricket that was, if possible, an even paler shade of green than the first made these.

Another major contributor to the general din of the Upper Sonoran night was a kind of grasshopper, or katydid. It wasn't the kind of grasshopper you would see flying through a sunlit meadow though. This grasshopper was mottled pink and brown like the endpapers of a Victorian novel. Its wings were pathetic little tabs, useless for flying. Because a helmetlike arrangement extends back from the head to cover these wings, it is called a shield-backed grasshopper. The stridulations made by its little wings are a very fair imitation of maracas: "Zeet-zeet-zeet . . . Zeet-zeet-zeet . . . Zeet-zeet-zeet. . . ."

Soon after the grasshoppers started, the first stars came out as if to dance to the orthopteran orchestra. In the south Jupiter shone bright and green. One of the brighter stars of the constellation Draco appeared directly overhead, and the handle of the Big Dipper (which is not itself a constellation, but part of Ursa Major, the Great Bear) was visible in the northwest. The dark side of the moon could also be seen, a purple patch against the violet sky. This was still the dense air of lower altitude, though, so even the brightest stars wavered and blinked.

The Beetle Eaters

When all the crickets and grasshoppers in the canyon had begun to stridulate, the din was enough to drown out subtler sounds like the trickle of water—the creek still ran above ground in parts of the canyon—or the rustle of movement in the grass. The owl in the laurel was not confused by the noise, though, and she could use it as a source of information. If the crickets in one place stopped singing, she knew something was there.

She was not as alert as she would be later. The mice, wood rats, and rabbits were afraid to come into the open when the moon was up. But when the crickets around a rocky place farther down the streambed fell silent, she turned her head to stare into the deep rock shadows. She didn't see anything, and the crickets started up again in a few minutes, so she blinked and then turned away to watch a pallid bat as it fluttered along the canyon wall.

The large bat was looking for crickets and beetles among the stones. As with most bats, his vision was fairly good, and he often hunted the large insects preferred by his species on the ground, where echolocation isn't effective. (Echolocation only works in the air and many large insects seldom fly.) He was unusual in appearance, even for a bat, with yellowish fur and ears so long they might almost have served as a second pair of wings. His long ears are an adaptation to hot nights—numerous blood vessels throughout their thin skin radiated excess heat into the air.

Luckily for him he didn't find anything near the owl's roost. She was glad to take bats, if she could get them. After he flew away, she felt restless. Quietly watching potential prey was frustrating, especially when her stomach was empty. So on hearing a faint splash in the part of the creekbed where the crickets had stopped singing, she flew down in that direction to investigate.

A large raccoon, bored with eating the carrion beetles he had found swarming around some excrement in the creekbed, was attempting to catch juicy tadpoles in a little basin underneath a dry waterfall. Beetles are the most numerous insects in the world, but not the tastiest. He had just closed his paw on a tadpole when he felt a disturbance in the air above his head and looked up. Two staring eyes glided silently past

20

above him. He jumped backwards, but the owl was already on her way down the canyon, heading toward the pasture that the hawk had flown over at sunset. She knew better than to attack a full-grown raccoon.

The startled raccoon put his head down and ran into the trees. Since he wasn't taking his usual care not to step on dry leaves and twigs, he made a lot of noise. He moved surprisingly fast for such a rotund-looking animal. When he reached a patch of brush he calmed down, and the noise stopped abruptly—so abruptly, in fact, that it was almost as though he had vanished. But he had only started to pick his way with care again. The canyon fell back into its moonlit stillness.

It wasn't the first time the raccoon had encountered the owl, of course. They had been neighbors for years, having established territories in the canyon at about the same time. He was used to the deep tolling of her calls in the twilight; she was part of his world. The fact that she had eaten several of his offspring over the years didn't prejudice him against her since his interest in procreation stopped at the act of mating. If he had been able to rationalize his lack of paternal feeling, he might even have been pleased—fewer raccoons meant less competition in the long run. Anyway, he had managed to grab an owlet or two that had ventured forth prematurely from the fissure in a cliff where the owl nested up the canyon.

But there had been no opportunity for that this year. The owl's mate had been shot by some jacklighting deer poachers in the fall, so there hadn't been any owlets. There wasn't any shortage of male great horned owls in the vicinity, but she was about the oldest, fiercest owl around; and the young males that had been attracted by her calls in the winter were simply too clumsy or intimidated to mate with her successfully.

In the total darkness of a tunnel through thick brush, the raccoon sat back on his haunches and sniffed the air. Under the sun he seemed an amusing sort of creature, but in the darkness that hid the clever paws and rakish mask, there was nothing clownish about him. A flashlight directed into the brush that hid him would have picked out two eyes as burning and yellow as any mountain lion's. And something morose and manipulative in his temperament gave him a certain capacity for malevolence. Smelling nothing of particular interest, he dropped down on all fours and moved in the direction of a manzanita thicket covered with ripe berries farther up the canyon wall.

Spider Eyes

The stillness in the canyon was an illusion. There is always movement where there is food, although that movement may be measurable in inches rather than in yards. The small world that the raccoon had been exploiting proceeded with its affairs. The fat black beetles ate, blundered into the basin, and were eaten by the beetles that lived in the water. Shriveled orange leaves from an overhanging buckeye fell one by one onto the dried algae of the rocks. A faint pungency of ammonia hung in the air from the rotting matter that attracted the insects.

Although the swarming beetles were the most conspicuous creatures in this world, they didn't seem to be the dominant ones. They were too clumsy and random in their movements, as indeed were most of the other insects—moths, mosquitoes, or gnats. All were easy prey to the spiders that waited everywhere to catch them in nets: at the bottom of holes, on the ground, or even over the water. The eyes of even the most rapacious wasp or dragonfly have a certain randomness. Their multifaceted structure makes them seem blank and obtuse. But the predatory sentience of the mildest spider is plain in its eyes. (Most species have eight.) They are hard, black little chips of awareness that seem oddly familiar on a body quite alien to us in most other ways.

The moon over the canyon reflected on hundreds of these eyes, and hundreds of others were there, hidden from its light. The rock walls of the bank were dotted with round, tentlike webs, and in the middle of each—upside-down—sat a black and white striped spider called a sheetweb weaver because its web is like a sheet. Bundles of mummified insects dangled from most of the webs, and one of the weavers was just then pulling a moth into her tent. Only the daddy longlegs that stalked everywhere over the rock walls seemed able to touch the webs without getting caught in them.

In a grassy spot above the rocky bank, a slender, sand-colored spider crouched inside a funnel of silk spun into a dirt cranny. Her eyes were set in two rows at the front of her head, but like the sheet weavers and most other kinds of web-living spiders, she didn't use them for spotting her prey. She could tell by touch which part of her web was being stirred by a captive. Whenever anything landed on the web, she ran straight toward it, following the vibration of the strands. She used her eyes to watch for enemies—large, moving shadows beyond the web. If one appeared, she would retire into the depth of the funnel. The funnel weaver's neighbor, a little gray *Tidarren* spider that lived in an irregular web stretched across a branch of an oak sapling above the grass, used the same warning system, although instead of a funnel she retreated to a rolled-up leaf.

Not all spiders live in webs. The striped, gray spiders called wolf spiders that run over the rocks and sand of the streambed use their eyes to catch food. Four of the wolf spider's eyes are small, like the eyes of web spiders, but the other four are much larger and glow green in a flashlight as if these were indeed tiny wolves. This shine is caused, as in other nocturnal creatures, by a layer of reflective material behind the visual cells of the retina. When the light has passed through and stimulated the visual cells once, it is reflected by this layer so that it passes back through the cells and stimulates them again. The brain receives double the information it would have without the layer and makes a correspondingly clearer picture.

Like other free-ranging predators, the wolf spiders are more selective in their choice of prey than the sedentary web spiders. They don't spring at anything that wanders within reach, and this trait makes them seem gentler than their fellow arachnids. One stood motionless a few inches from the beetle horde while a kind of pygmy daddy longlegs, called a laniatore, walked right under her jaws. Unmolested, the laniatore (which was a beautiful shade of coral) continued on his way, furiously waving his sensitive second pair of legs like a portly gentleman laying about before him with his cane in a dark alley.

Flea Bites

As the night wore on, the residue of energy from the day's sunlight dwindled. Photosynthetic activity gradually slowed in the darkened leaves. The mosquitoes and other flying insects aroused by the sunset sank back to the branches and ground. The pipistrelle bats had eaten their fill (some had eaten so much that their stomachs were distended) and flew back to the rock crevices in which they roosted. As the returning bats hung themselves up on the walls of their roosts, baby bats that had been hiding in crannies scuttled out and climbed on their mothers to nurse.

The bats and the owl weren't the only night flyers. A poor-will, western cousin of the whip-poor-will, opened his gigantic mouth to scoop a late mosquito out of the air above the canyon, then sideslipped, folded his long, narrow wings, and dropped into the darkness downstream from the owl's laurel. He landed softly on the bare floor of a live oak grove, seemingly a vulnerable place to rest, but his plumage matched the pattern of the leaf litter. Another poor-will called upstream—a plaintive, diffident sound that expressed the secretness of the darkness just as the scrub jays' cocky squawks expressed the naked sunlight of the slopes. The bird in the oaks lifted and flexed his wings but made no answer.

The moon had passed its zenith just after sunset. As it sank behind the oak trees, it cast slanting rays of light that silvered the dusty air and made the parched woodland appear lush and romantic. Moonlit patches of rock and foliage took on illusory shapes and seemed to leap out of the darkness. One of these shapes—in the daytime a tangle of poison oak and wild grape vines on a little delta where a side gully entered the canyon—was particularly bizarre. A peculiar sound came from it, as though a roll-up window blind like those still found in cheap hotels had snapped up suddenly to spin around on its rod: "Rattle, rattle, slap."

The sound stopped, but started up again when an identical sound came from inside the oak grove. Then the owl called from the pasture, and both sounds ceased abruptly. The owl's call also frightened a brush mouse, and fallen leaves rustled slightly as she ran for cover in the vines. She raced under them until she came to a pile of twigs that leaned against an ancient fence post. There she vanished underground.

Certain things about this pile of twigs set it apart from the accumulations of debris left by the winter floods. Most of the twigs were about the same length, and they were piled in a conical shape like an old-fashioned beehive. Six inconspicuous holes opened into it—three near the bottom, two on the sides, one on top. The real proof that the pile was an inhabited structure was even less conspicuous. Around some of the holes, little gray mites hung on the twigs, and, in the chambers to which the tunnels led, uncomfortable numbers of fleas hopped and crawled.

The hot nights of July are the best time for flea breeding, and the population in this nest had already been building up for several years. Two occupants of the tunnels didn't mind the fleas though. In fact the fleas might have been one of the reasons they had moved in. The Pacific tree frog that was spending the hot season in one of the lower tunnels ate quantities of them, and the alligator lizard that spent her nights in the tunnels enjoyed an occasional one. Since neither was a mammal, the fleas weren't able to return the compliment. The brush mouse that had disappeared under the pile didn't actually live in the tunnels but had a nest of her own underneath them, so she too was free from the flea population explosion.

The only resident of the pile that really minded the fleas was its owner and partial builder (he had put on a new roof after occupying it in the fall), a dusky-footed wood rat. Crouching in a nest carefully lined with willow leaves and thistledown near the center of the pile, he was running out of patience. The fur of his neck and back was thin and mangy from repeated fleabites, and he could hardly take a step in his larder or privy without getting more. He forgot the owl and, lifting his tail, vibrated it fast and hard against the twigs of the nest entrance. This was the source of the roll-up sound. It was a gratifyingly loud noise and relieved his feelings somewhat, but it didn't drive the fleas away. It worked on other rats, even on some snakes, but the fleas weren't intimidated.

He picked up a poison oak leaf and started to eat it, but had to drop it almost immediately when a bite on his hind leg made him turn around. They were invading his nest now. He couldn't bear it any more. He bit his leg—missing the flea—squealed in frustration, and rushed out of the nest into the tunnel.

Hurrying along the dark tunnel, he caught the smell of a *Calosoma* ground beetle. These large black beetles are no danger to wood rats, but the rats are terrified of them for some reason. He heard the scraping sounds of the beetle ambling around the corner toward him, and the hair on his back stood up, but he was so irritated that he kept moving. Feeling the beetle's presence in the pitch blackness, he lunged forward nervously. The startled insect exuded an acrid substance from her abdomen which stung the rat's eyes and nose and drove him back down the tunnel. He had to take another way out. Finally reaching an exit hole, he paused with one forepaw against his chest. The moon was setting.

A wolf spider stood motionless a few inches from a beetle horde, while a kind of pygmy daddy longlegs walked right under her jaws.

He was an attractive animal, quite unlike the Norway rat of cities. His fur was soft—grayish brown on the back and sides, white on the belly—and it covered his tail. His eyes were large and lustrous and, as he looked around cautiously, they seemed more expressive than the eyes of other rodents. This was because he moved them in their sockets. Most rodents have spherical lenses in their eyes which focus an image equally well from any direction and therefore don't need to be moved in the socket. But a wood rat's lens is flattened like a human's and can only be focused from one direction at a time, so it has to be movable.

As soon as the moon was down, he left the vines and hurried along a path that had been carefully cleared of leaves, twigs, and anything else that might rustle or snap. He didn't like making noise in his movements or passing through patches of moonlight. The path led to a recently fallen live oak. The demise of the oak had raised the value of the property quite a bit by rat standards, since running along the smooth trunk made almost no noise. At the other end of the trunk a clump of willows grew in the sandy soil of the gully.

The willows served the wood rat as lumberyard and grocery store since he could either eat the leaves, twigs, and bark or use them as building materials. But when he reached them, he needed to do some things before getting to work. First he scratched his flea-bitten back in the sand and groomed his whiskers and stomach. Then he ran to the far edge of the clump and urinated to discourage his noisy neighbor in the grove from trying to exploit it. After that he felt better, so he ate a few leaves. Then he began stripping leaves and bark off the trees.

When he had a mouthful, he followed the path back to his house. Instead of returning to the flea-infested nest, however, he turned into a side passage that ran up to the upper center of the house, ending there at a cave-in. Beyond the cave-in was the nest of the previous occupant of the house, who was still there, in fact, in a mummified form that testified to the watertightness of the roof. The summer before, she had succumbed to a parasitic blood disease contracted from the fleas.

The wood rat wasn't aware that he lived in a mausoleum and would have been unimpressed if he had been. What interested him about the passage was the fact that it had been empty for a long time and, there-fore, contained no fleas. He set about widening the dead end to make a new nest for himself.

The Parasite Tree

After the wood rat ran away, the ground beetle in the tunnel stood for several minutes without moving anything except her antennae and mouth parts. She rotated these to the same purpose that a dog sniffs—to sample the molecules of the air and ground. Finally sensing no further disturbance, she turned her back on the rat smell and returned the way she had come, down the tunnel.

Something was urging her to leave the darkness of the rat house where she had spent the daylight hours. Perhaps it was a tiny quantity of hormone released into her nervous system in response to subtle changes of the earth's electromagnetic field after sunset. Nobody really knows. In any case, she obeyed the summons without haste. Ground beetles have a reputation for quickness, but this individual was not behaving typically. She moved at a creaking amble, perhaps ill or injured, perhaps simply a slow individual. She covered considerable ground anyway.

Five minutes or so after the wood rat had emerged, the ground beetle came out of a hole at the other side of the nest. Her eyes registered the starlight, but she didn't pause as had the wood rat—she was no safer inside than outside. This was demonstrated by two tooth marks on the rear of her abdomen which the brush mouse under the house had given her a few days before. She was almost impossible to see in the dark any-way, and she made little noise with her deliberate, long-legged gait.

She threaded her way through the vine tangle and into the oak grove, passing seed-laden harvester ants, a couple of daddy longlegs, and a field cricket. Arriving at the foot of a small oak, she started up its trunk. She often climbed trees, and tonight she was fortunate because this tree was slowly dying. Moribund trees tend to be full of parasitic organisms, so she would have no trouble meeting prey. She passed some of these parasites as she climbed. The sporophores of rainbow shelf fungus stuck out of the trunk like ornamental cornices. She had to climb over or around them. Every year the fungus grew deeper into the living wood of the tree, assisted by the maggotlike larvae of long-horned beetles. The larvae ate tunnels through the wood, carrying the spores of the fungus into the tree's heart. Adult long-horned beetles, dark brown and thin-bodied, paused from grazing on the outer bark and directed their antennae toward the ground beetle, but her acrid smell faded as she moved on up the tree, and they went back to feeding.

She reached the crotch of the tree and started into the foliage. Above, a big orb-weaver spider spun around in the center of her sixteen-inch, geometrical web, following the movements of a small fly. When the fly finally touched the web, the spider darted toward it, but the fly blundered out again. The orb weaver returned to the web's center. When the beetle passed over the branch to which the upper part of the web was anchored, the spider felt the disturbance and became apprehensive. She worked her legs quickly up and down, making the web vibrate. Web and maker disappeared in a blur of motion.

The beetle paid no attention. She had come upon a trail—traces of sweetish, sticky stuff on the limb—and, although she wasn't moving any faster, she was following it. It led toward the end of a leafy branch. A certain distance along the branch, she began to feel infinitesimal vibrations through her feet. When the vibrations stopped, she stopped. Here an advantage of her sedateness became clear. Her prey, a green looper caterpillar on a leaf stalk, had no defense except its ability to let go of its perch and drop out of the tree. But it could do this quickly, so the beetle needed to approach without making vibrations that would disturb the caterpillar. She proceeded quietly until she was leaning over her quarry as if she meant to kiss instead of catch it.

The caterpillar sensed the faint movement of the beetle's jaws and curled itself up, but the jaws had closed. They were formidable jaws. The beetle lifted the looper clear of the leaf and started to retrace her steps down the branch to a place where it could be safely eaten. In the surrounding branches, the tree crickets stridulated with deafening gusto. The hotter it is, the louder and faster tree crickets sing. This was an unusually hot night so this background music had a faint edge of hysteria, as though a feverish conductor were trying to lead his orchestra through a two-hour piece in one hour.

A male tree cricket was disturbed by the ground beetle's downward passage and jumped to another branch which happened to hold a female of his species. For several moments the two crawled about the branch, apparently at random. When they eventually came into contact, the male raised his wings, stridulated, and backed up aggressively toward the female. She retreated from his overtures several times, but he finally forced her to climb on his back. Discovering the hedonic gland between his wings, she began to feed on its tantalizing secretions.

Quite suddenly the female bent her swordlike ovipositer around under the male's abdomen. When she straightened it again a few seconds later, a tiny, reddish bead hung from the rear of her abdomen. This was the spermatophore—a syringelike structure full of sperm which the male had implanted during their brief copulation. For the next fifteen minutes the male kept the female on his back—no easy task as she kept losing interest in the hedonic gland and climbing off. When she did this, he stridulated energetically and backed up at her until she remounted. Meanwhile the red bead was contracting and dilating, pumping its load of sperm into the female. At last the male let the female go, at first following her a little way with quick, excited movements as if expostulating on her coyness. Then he turned and climbed upward, while the female crawled down the branch. As she descended, the female stopped twice to curl the tip of her abdomen to her mouth, finally succeeding in eating the red bead. Then she crawled into a bunch of leaves and was still. The male stopped at the end of the branch, wings lowered, silent.

The Storm's Shadow

The next time the wood rat came out of his house, when the Big Dipper had set behind the north wall of the canyon, he had a pleasant surprise. A high wall of clouds had moved in to blot out the stars of the western sky, and it was even darker than before. The clouds were thunderheads, although only a few weak, pink flashes of the distant lightning reached the foothills. He hurried off confidently along his path, leaving behind a small cloud of dust in the dry, still air. He could move quickly because he didn't depend on his eyes but on habit-formed memories of the exact movements required to follow the path—a kind of choreographic map of his territory. The only drawback to this system was that if some accident took him off the routes marked on the map, he could become lost. Then, even if he was only a few yards from his house, he would have to wander around until he ran into something familiar again.

The shadow of the storm pleased him especially because it gave him the nerve to climb trees which he was afraid to do in moonlight or bright starlight. He liked to climb trees because he could move more quickly and quietly among the branches than on the ground. He went up a spindly little laurel, then crossed over to a bushier oak. A roosting rufous-sided towhee fluttered away in his path, startling him, and a shield-backed grasshopper stopped stridulating and dived for the ground as the rat's weight bent the bough it sat on. Actually it had little to fear from the vegetarian wood rat, who preferred such delicacies as poison oak or nightshade berries to animal food.

A moment later, when a screech owl called from the gully, the rat prudently followed the grasshopper to the ground. Although the little owl's largest prey was mice, his call was more unnerving than the great horned owl's. He sounded like a maniacal, toothless old woman shouting, "Watch out!" two or three times, then going into a gale of squeaky laughter. The rat hid under a toyon bush, watching the darkness for a sign of movement and applying his nose and ears to the gathering of more precise information.

He caught a smell of the other rat that lived up the hill, and it annoyed him, although he had felt differently during the breeding season a few months before. The other rat was a female. He had visited her a few times then, although an older, bigger rat that lived in a gigantic nest in a poison oak thicket downstream had usually reached her first. It had been exciting, but she didn't appeal to him at the moment. Lately there seemed to be an excessive number of young rats wandering around, and he had to spend a tedious amount of time driving them out of his house when they tried to move in. So he was very much concerned with defending his property.

He heard a sound from the direction of his nest and ran back full of aggression. Instead of a newly weaned wood rat, however, he found the tail end of a gopher snake protruding from the main entrance to the twig pile. He stopped with his ears back, a posture of alarm; but after a while when the tail didn't seem to have any designs on him—didn't move at all in fact—his ears came forward again. He began to approach it.

Gopher snakes habitually crawl into holes, and this individual had acted typically on encountering the rat's nest with its many entrances. Inside he had found the scent or taste—since he used his tongue—of the wood rat and had followed it to a place where it was particularly strong. Since no greater stimulus was offered, he had then remained where he was until he felt a pain at the tip of his tail. The rat had bitten him.

The tail coiled around, inadvertently catching the rat in a reflex loop. As the snake withdrew down the tunnel, the rat was dragged toward the hole. He squealed in fear and struggled as the coil tightened, but then rat and tail got stuck at the entrance, so the tail uncoiled and disappeared. The rat ran off and climbed the nearest tree. A few minutes later, a gray fox that had been attracted by the squeals appeared at the edge of the vines. She lowered her head and whined to see if she could provoke some movement, but the wood rat stayed frozen in the branches. The fox sniffed the ground, glanced over her shoulder, and padded away.

Inside the rat's nest, the snake lay quiet for a time. When he started to move again, he passed the alligator lizard that was in an alcove off the tunnel. Since the snake's striking reflexes required thermal stimulus, he ignored the cold-blooded lizard. The fleas hopped up excitedly as he passed but landed back on the chamber floor, unrewarded. They also sought warm-blooded prey. The snake found the way out and crawled away. When the rat finally came down from the tree, he carefully renewed his scent markings around the house before he entered again.

The Unwound Clock

With midnight left behind, the darkness seemed prolonged out of proportion to the twilight hours. It was as though time, which is based on the sun's movement through the sky, had begun to lose its hold on the world. Very little happened to encourage a belief that the universe was proceeding forward into the future. The stars spun gradually overhead and the planets pursued their own subtle orbits, neither providing much impression of orderly celestial movement. It is hard to imagine the Milky Way leading anywhere.

A rufous-sided towhee fluttered away in the wood rat's path, and a shield-backed grasshopper dived for the ground.

It seemed, at this time of night, that it might always be dark. Sounds suffered the same distortion as time. Flattened by the dense air of the canyon, the voices of coyotes calling from the top of the chaparral ridge drifted down as weird, spiraling sounds instead of the high, doglike barks and howls coyotes really make. The poor-will cries began to sound like water dripping into deep, echoing pools, and the insects' unflagging stridulations fell in and out of strange rhythms and syncopations as the different songs overlapped or drew apart.

The air was thinner on the slopes above the canyon, but it also moved around more, making it difficult to tell where sounds or smells came from. The murmur of water from the canyon would suddenly be cut off by the whisper of digger pine branches moving on a rocky knoll a hundred feet away. Hot blasts of dust and aromatic chaparral resins alternated with the cooler smells of laurel leaves and damp sand from below.

Events emerged from the dark with a certain unexpectedness. A toad hopped across a dirt road with a small, yellow scorpion clamped in its jaws, the poisonous stinger curled alongside the toad's black, unconcerned eye. The sound of heavy breathing from a ridgetop path through the chaparral grew louder, and a small deer appeared, almost winded, galloping in panic from something in the darkness below. Passing a tree, she frightened some band-tailed pigeons from their roosts. The birds flew higher in the tree with a loud clapping of wings that stopped as abruptly as it had begun. Such events lacked continuity. They were random streaks and chips on the hard surface of darkness, heat, and cricket monologues —a surface like that of a scratched phonograph record patiently and interminably repeating itself under a sticking needle.

False Dawn

The horned owl sat in a cottonwood tree beside the star-thistle pasture. She had just finished eating a brush rabbit that had made the mistake of venturing out of its streamside thicket into the open. All that remained of it—jaws and bits of fur—lay at the bottom of the tree. The owl watched a striped skunk approach the tree, sniffing the ground like a dog and quite oblivious to anything watching him. (A skunk will come up to a man at night and sniff around his feet without bothering to stop and look up.) He found the remains of the rabbit, but there was nothing left to eat, so he moved off—a lucky skunk. The owl would have eaten him if she had been hungry, since horned owls are insensitive to skunk smell.

The clouds that had obscured the western stars were breaking up, but there seemed at times to be more light in the sky than the reemergence of some stars could account for. It was not a steady light, perhaps only a glow, perhaps not even that. It was impossible to be sure if the sky was lighter or not. The stars were as brilliant as ever, but the trunks of the little oak trees on the grassy hills seemed to stand out more clearly against the ground.

The crickets didn't think the night was ending and continued stridulating. But a few birds woke up and squawked hoarsely once or twice. The owl began to call too. A little later the strange light disappeared, if it had ever been at all. The birds went back to sleep, but the owl continued to call. The source of this spectral light, sometimes called *false dawn*, is not known. It may be sunlight reflected from meteor bands.

Ephemeral as it was, the light seemed to lift the spell under which the night had fallen. Mosquitoes began to whine around the streambed again, and bats reappeared over the chaparral and trees. Another pallid bat, flying along the creekbed where it bordered the meadow, found a Jerusalem cricket crawling over the sand. He landed and rushed at the cricket. He could move surprisingly fast over the ground, scuttling along on folded wings. The cricket, heavily armored and without wings, reared up on its hind legs in a defensive posture. With its large, round head, it looked like a tiny dwarf in a suit of bronze armor.

37

But the bat made short work of the cricket, darting in to bite it in half. Then he listened for a moment to see if the disturbance had attracted any attention. All was quiet, so he began to gulp down the cricket's abdomen. When the owl called again, he started nervously and flew off, leaving the head and legs. "Hoo HOO hoo hoo hoo," she cried, ruffling her feathers slightly on the accented syllable. Later during the fall mating season, the canyon would be full of owl calls, but she was the only one calling this time.

In the boulder-strewn hills above the pasture, a big, rufous male coyote loped down a grassy slope and disappeared into a stand of oaks and digger pines. A few moments later a much smaller female with yellowish fur appeared above the slope. She was a slight individual with a thin coat, a ratty tail, and a stiff hind leg, but like the male she moved with delicate assurance over the rough terrain. She paused motionless on the slope for several minutes. Suddenly a black-tailed jackrabbit emerged from a nearby clump of chaparral and ran in the direction that the male coyote had taken. There were slight rustling sounds as the jackrabbit's hind feet kicked into the leaf litter, but the coyotes' running was virtually noiseless. The female made no attempt to catch the jackrabbit but moved off parallel to its course after it had disappeared into the trees. She knew it would run in a circle in order to stay within its known range, so she was in no hurry. The jackrabbit, too, ran without great haste. The hunt was so quiet and diffident that its mortal implications seemed dreamlike, remote, and very innocent.

The Dusty Threshold

A female ground cricket threaded her way among the pebbles and dry stalks at the edge of the creekbed, moving in the general direction of a male singing nearby. His voice sounded similar to high-pitched bursts of radio static and, unlike the tree crickets, he sang only at scattered intervals as if he felt insecure on the ground. These were unremarkable, brown crickets, smaller than the other cricket species that lived in the foothills.

The female cricket came to an obstacle and stopped. The drying clay had cracked to form a deep fissure several inches across in her path. A pale pink glow emanated from it, dimly illuminating the stems of the plants at its edge. In the cricket's compound vision, the soft glow broke up into a grid of light, fading to darkness at the edges. It attracted her, and she moved toward its center so that she was peering over the edge of the fissure.

Blobs of brighter light appeared in the middle of the grid, attached to an elongated blob of darkness which, as the cricket watched, began to move deeper into the fissure, pulling the light blobs along with it. The female glowworm that had been waiting for the flying males of her species (actually a kind of beetle) to be attracted by her light had become alarmed at the appearance of the cricket's waving antennae and shiny head that reflected her glow in a somewhat baleful fashion. So she withdrew into the fissure with her light, a phosphorescent substance under the chitin of the last few segments of her abdomen.

The cricket didn't move for several minutes after the light went out, as if the encounter had made her forget her original purpose. The male didn't call again. He had crawled under a rock. The hilltops on the eastern side of the pasture, which had appeared pale from the reflection of the starlight on the yellow grass, seemed to darken now as the sky above them turned milky. The ground cricket started to walk around the fissure, but when she was almost at the end she hesitated and crawled down into it instead.

As the details of leaves and grass began to emerge, colored a uniform shade of blue, the tree crickets continued to sing. In fact they seemed to increase their tempo a little. It was as hot and dry as it had been earlier. The owl in the cottonwood blinked and glared up at the paling sky.

At about the time the Milky Way disappeared, a round shape detached itself from one of the ground squirrel burrows, spread speckled, pointed wings, and flew to a fence post at the edge of the pasture. It landed on a pair of long legs that seemed out of proportion to its body and stood on the post, bobbing up and down occasionally. It was a burrowing owl, one of a pair that was nesting in the abandoned squirrel burrow. This species is as likely to be active during the day as at night.

When the sky above the eastern hills became red, the insect din stopped, first in the open spaces and soon afterward in the canyons and shady spots. In the spell of silence that followed, the horned owl flew back up the canyon to the laurel tree. Secure in its shadows, she shook her feathers out and preened her wings. Then she regurgitated a gray pellet of indigestible material—fur, skin, and bits of bone—leaning over solemnly to watch as it fell through the branches. It bounced on an exposed root and came to rest among the scattering of other pellets that had accumulated under the tree.

All the scrub jays in the foothills seemed to wake up at once, making the same raucous, interrogative noises that they had been making at dusk the night before. Dawn was not a gradual process here. Right after the jays' explosion of calls, the chaparral filled with scratching and squawks as the towhees, thrashers, and other insect eaters hurried to fill their stomachs before it became too hot. The grasslands looked deceptively frosty in the morning light, but the temperature was already climbing with the sun. The burrowing owl flew off his post to pursue the large, band-winged grasshoppers that had just become active. Catching one, he disappeared into the burrow with it. Later the owlets would emerge to teeter and gawk at the burrow entrance.

A California quail called peevishly, impatient with a nearly full-grown brood that was increasingly hard to keep together. He looked up and saw the red-tailed hawk coming down the canyon, gave an alarm call, and ran into the brush without trying to drive the others ahead of him as he would have a few weeks earlier. The hawk landed on the overhanging digger pine and watched the red sunlight climb down to the canyon floor. By the time the light reached the creekbed, it wasn't red anymore. Dawn was over.

As the bear waited, the shimmering tide of moonlight ebbed away up the gulch, and a more substantial darkness arose to replace it.

PART TWO
The Sugar Pine

The Sugar Pine

For trees, you see, rather conceal themselves in daylight.
They reveal themselves only after sunset.
Algernon Blackwood, "The Man the Trees Loved"

ON A JULY AFTERNOON the chaparral-covered ridges are even hotter than the foothills. They lack even the dubious shade of the small oaks, and the streambeds are inaccessible at the bottom of steep, brush-covered canyon walls. The brushy slopes are like an endless inferno, but there is an end. Running along the ridgetop is a rim of green, darker than the olive drab of the brush, where the chaparral belt ends as it began—in patches—indicating a change in soil patterns. As the thin clay of the ridge gives way to the deeper, yellowish loam of the Klamath plateau, the chaparral plants are shaded out by the dark rim: the forest of the Transition zone.

It is a dry, spare forest. Ponderosa pines and incense cedars grow in open stands on a mat of needles that is bare and dusty in July. Only in shaded gullies and hollows do denser stands of white fir, big-leaf maple, golden-cup oak, and California black oak grow. Even so, it is a great change to move from the chaparral into the shade of the pines. Under the dustiest, most sun-blasted trees at the edge of the forest there is a breeze and a faint tinge of ice in the air that is entirely absent under the blue oaks of the foothills.

A few hours before the red-tailed hawk frightened the ground squirrels in the foothill pasture, a peculiar black bear sat against one of the trees at the forest's edge idly eating carpenter ants and looking with a certain degree of amazement at the shade. He was about half bear-size and thin enough to be a dog. He was small because he was half grown and thin because his mother had recently disowned him, and he wasn't yet adept at getting food. The peculiar thing about this bear was his fur. On his head and legs it was typically black and glossy, but it grew from his back and sides in long mottled patches of reddish blonde, as if he had been doused with a mixture of peroxide and hair grower. The tendency toward color mutations in black bears is well known; cinnamon-furred black bears are common in California, and striped and spotted individuals have been reported. But this bear seemed to have reached for the limits of aberrance.

He looked at the cool forest shade with surprise because he hadn't known before that morning there was anything else. Since his mother had driven him off, he had wandered around more or less at random. Nobody had told him that black bears stay in the forest. The previous night he had followed a canyon so far that, looking up from the ground on which he had been tracing an intriguing sequence of smells, he noticed that there were no trees at all on the slopes above. He had been in open places before this, but the shaggy shapes of pine or fir had always been nearby.

He had sniffed at this new arrangement of things suspiciously, but the intriguing new odors in the air made him linger despite his uneasiness. Then events had distracted him. A porcupine appeared, another straggler from the woods whose greeting—raised quills and a taciturn grunt—had been familiar enough. He had found ripe manzanita berries and had spent a long time stripping the branches of them, savoring their sweet sourness at the back of his tongue. But after the sun had come up, the place had begun to lose its fascination. Neither the digger pines nor the chaparral plants afforded enough shade for an animal as large and black as a bear, and the ground, so interestingly bare and dusty in the dark, had begun to scorch even his tough paws. He had retreated back upstream along the canyon until he saw dark silhouettes topping its walls; then he pulled himself up the steep slopes of scrub oak until he reached them. His slimness was deceptive; he was already stronger than a man.

He was thirsty, so when some Steller's jays—the crested, indigo jays of conifer forests—found him and began to scold, he left the glare of the forest's edge and moved deeper into the trees. He walked the length of the ridge, sniffing around the gullies for a spring and listening for the trickle of water under the hissing of wind through pine needles. But it was only a spur ridge. He would have to move farther into the mountains along the maze of logging roads that covered the ridgetops to find water.

The Sweet Place

Deep in the forest, a spring burst from under a ridgetop and made a steep little meadow on a pocket of black, marshy soil, then rushed away down a gully. This soil oozed and bubbled with the icy water from under the mountains and was covered with blossoming hosackia—a native relative of clover with violet-yellow flowers—and studded with clumps of leopard lily, corn lily, and bleeding heart. The bright green of these plants could be seen for a long way through the dusty woods.

Being nearsighted and at least partly colorblind, the bear didn't see the green, but he smelled the spring even before it was visible through the trees. The scent of wet earth and vegetation—pollen, nectar, and the transpiration of water-rich leaves—was easy to distinguish from that of pine resin. He quickened his pace along the road he'd been following and started to run when he reached an abandoned track that cut across the top of the meadow. At the spring he paused to enjoy the coolness of the mud on his paws and took a long drink at a puddle.

Then he sidled over to a warm spot and sat on his multicolored rump. The conversation of a pair of ravens flying along the canyon below drifted to his ears, carried on a gentle breeze. It was just the right kind of breeze for smelling—warm and moist—and the bear opened his nostrils wide to get all the nuances. The lazy buzzing of flies and bumblebees called up pleasant associations of grubs and honey. A few inches from his hind paws a red, white, and gray *Phidippus* jumping spider, a daytime spider, ambled contentedly through the dust and twigs.

These raptures were interrupted by a mountain quail, as young and disheveled as the bear, who trotted out from behind a manzanita bush at the edge of the trees and appeared to succumb to an attack of hiccups. He jumped and squawked in evident distress, the clownish bobbing of his long head plume contributing to his drunken aspect. He was actually trying to scare the bear away from the clearing, but his performance only served to remind the intruder of a breakfast of quail eggs his mother had once provided. After listening to several minutes of denunciation, the bear rose and walked toward the manzanita bush. The quail shut up and scuttled into the woods, driving before him a whole tribe of variously aged relatives, all chattering at once in the voluble way of their species.

Not finding quail eggs, the bear wandered over to a pine stump on a knoll beside the meadow where carpenter ants with reddish fuzz on their black abdomens toiled around the entrance to their nest. The bear thought perhaps he might raid this nest. A little gray fence lizard rushed around the stump out of his way as he thrust his snout down to sniff at the hole. He smelled the tender white grubs in their larval chambers at the bottom of the hole and began to rake away the earth between the roots of the stump. But the nest was protected by a large root, and after awhile he grew tired of clawing and chewing at it, contenting himself instead with licking up the aroused hordes of soldiers and workers that swarmed out among the bits of yellow green wolf lichen and orange cedar mistletoe littering the ground.

Like the creekbeds of the foothills, the spring meadow was a locus of activity in an otherwise dry landscape. Now that the day was about to end, that activity increased. A golden-mantled ground squirrel, resembling an oversized chipmunk, ran out of the hosackia and began to forage on the small herbs of the knoll, biting off fuzzy seed capsules and stuffing them into her cheek pouches. A Douglas squirrel scolded from the treetops, and the sound of falling pinecone scales from the other side of the clearing indicated where another was at work. The colors in the clearing became brighter for a little while before the sun set. A dead pine on the middle of the knoll turned orange as the reddening light touched its brown needles. Three birds resting on its top—a junco and two creepers—turned orange with it.

Another junco, a purple finch, two western bluebirds, and a chipping sparrow converged on the puddle to drink, but all except the sparrow were nervous at the bear's presence and soon flew away. The sparrow took a leisurely drink, bathed, and then flew to the knoll, where he proceeded to pick at the herbs the ground squirrel had just left. A few Steller's jays called in the woods, but none appeared in the clearing. As the sun dropped below the treetops, isolated rays of light streaked across the hosackia and glittered on spider webs. A black and white bird—an Audubon's warbler—was fluttering through one of these shafts of fading light, chasing gnats.

After fading from the meadow, the sunlight colored the treetops briefly, then disappeared—the birds with it. The air cooled quickly as the damp which had been dissipated all day by the sun's heat rose from the meadow. Remnants of sun-warmed air stirred the trees, but the clearing was still. A chipmunk popped out of his burrow and rushed boldly to the top of the dead pine. Like the ground squirrels in the foothills, he wanted to find out what was going on before darkness fell. He saw the last sunlight touch the peaks to the southwest and gleam on the breast of a Cooper's hawk that flew past. The chipmunk flattened himself against the tree until the hawk was out of sight, then slipped back to the ground.

The increasing coolness stupefied the bees and flies; they dropped to the stems and leaves of the meadow plants and clung there, bowing them slightly with their weight. But the carpenter ants remained active, hurrying to repair the damage that the bear had done to their tunnel. Long lines of them ran back and forth from the succulent corn lilies, which provided a food supply in the form of honeydew exuded from the abdomens of green aphids that sucked the juices of the lilies. Many moths also fluttered around the lilies, attracted by the sweet smell of the white flower spikes.

A robin sang a few notes in the already dark forest as if to signal the end of the daytime sounds. A long-jawed orb weaver—an attenuated spider with a zebra-striped abdomen and carrot-colored jaws—sidled to the center of her web, which was nearly two feet wide and was built horizontally over the main channel of spring water. She crouched upside-down underneath the web, waiting for insects, who come to lay their eggs in the water, to land on top of it. She would catch them from below. A crane fly, looking like a giant mosquito, blundered into the web and out again before she could grab it. In the channel, the golden-bodied, black-headed scavenger beetles that had spent the daylight burrowing in the mud gyrated erratically. Water boatmen and striders that had been active throughout the day seemed indifferent to the darkness and kept on rowing about. Down on the mud bottom, hundreds of tiny, red, wormlike creatures stood on their tails, waving in the current like a bed of eelgrass and filtering nourishment from the water with microscopic gills.

A long-jawed orb weaver crouched upside-down underneath her web, waiting for insects, who come to lay their eggs in the water, to land on top of it.

These were the larvae of the gnats that the warbler had been chasing. Another larva, that of the caddis fly, crawled along a submerged pine needle. In the cylindrical case that it had made for itself out of rotten bark, it looked like an animated twig.

The stars began to come out, sparkling above the pine tops with a quiet authority they had lacked when seen through the denser air of the foothills. As if in deference to this authority, the clearing was hushed. There were no tree crickets in the pines and manzanita, and the ground crickets sang in scattered bursts that grew more and more infrequent as the temperature dropped. The only sustained sound was the whisper and chuckle of the spring.

Other species were indifferent to the higher altitude. A *Calosoma* ground beetle identical to the wood rat's visitor in the foothills loomed up out of a mouse hole and stalked off in search of a caterpillar. Wolf spiders patrolled the shores of the puddle on which floated, like petals, the white wings of pine looper moths that had fallen in and been eaten by the scavenger beetles. Multitudes of the pale moths clustered around the blossoms of western pennyroyal—drab violet flowers by day but strangely bright in the moonlight—or blundered into the traps set for them by gray cobweb-weaver spiders. A western toad, his black eyes lustrous and his skin the same color and texture as the ground, walked across the knoll.

The Haunted Road

Two fluttering gray forms chased each other down the meadow—little California bats that squeaked like mice while simultaneously making the faint, ticking sounds of echolocation. The bear cocked his ears and lifted his head as they went over; the squeaks reminded him of warm, crunchy things to eat. Nightfall stimulated him, and the meadow smelled even more enticing after dark when the damp air was loaded with exhalations.

He walked into the meadow vegetation and began to sample it as if it were a giant antipasto. First perhaps the hot juiciness of wild onions; then some lily bulbs, sweeter and starchier; next a few bees and ants, sour with formic acid. As he stood musing, a lily flower dangling from his snout, a meadow mouse scurried along one of the tiny paths that meandered through the hosackia and ran between his legs, unaware of his presence. The bear started and backed up to catch the mouse but stumbled and sat down rather heavily instead. He looked around for a moment, then suddenly jumped up and dashed into a grove of young firs at the bottom of the meadow. He was subject to panic if surprises happened to him, and the chilly mud of the meadow was unexpectedly disagreeable on his backside. The crashing sounds of his flight stopped suddenly, and the meadow became quiet except for a frog's croaking from the darkness below the fir grove. A young doe that had been waiting for the bear to go away came down to crop the meadow rushes, each of which had a bead of condensed moisture at its tip.

Following the spring through the firs, the bear snapped idly at a two-and-a-half-inch, long-horned beetle that buzzed past his ear. He didn't much like beetles; they were too dry and the large ones tended to get stuck in his throat. He found himself moving through a cloud of tiny moths, thousands of white needle-miners flying around the fir branches, waiting to lay their eggs on the needles that would provide food for their newly hatched larvae. Hundreds of equally tiny orb-weaver spiders worked busily on these branches, building miniature webs (which the morning breezes would tear apart) to catch the moths.

The bear emerged from the trees at a pool formed by the runoff of the spring before it passed under a logging road culvert. The frog that had been croaking beside it stopped. It was very dark here; the overhanging firs screened out the moon and most of the stars. The water was a chill, featureless black except when the two small bats that had passed the meadow earlier flew over it to drink, cutting shiny streaks in the surface with their tongues. The bear sniffed at the vague, fluttering shapes and ate—without much enthusiasm—a centipede that was crawling over the bare earth of the bank. The place didn't attract him.

He clambered up to the road and followed it downhill. It was an abandoned road, washed out and overgrown. The area had been logged years before, but the effects were still plain in the dry forest—stumps and bulldozer scars and bare spots sparsely grown with gooseberry and whitethorn. In the moonlight it was an eerie place. The pale soil of the road cuts and eroded gullies loomed overhead in weird shapes; young bushes crouched in the roadbed like skulking beasts; and the snags and piles of slash and uprooted stumps gleamed fitfully. The living trees looked skeletal in their isolation.

The young bear probably found nothing strange in these scars. He was used to them since most of California's ponderosa pine forest is in the same condition today. He moved along minding his business of sounds and smells. Luxuriant bunches of nettle and scarlet monkey-flower grew where springs crossed the road, and gray damselflies with golden reflective eyes rested on the wet earth and stones. They seemed to inhabit a spectral world of their own and weren't disturbed when the bear stepped only a few inches from them. A ground cricket stridulated in a fir grove but interrupted his song when the bear went past. In a rocky gully a Jerusalem cricket stridulated. He did this by rubbing his leg against his body, since he had no wings. It made an unmusical, scraping sound: "Dust. Dust. Dust." The sound of poor-will cries from the canyon below was even more hushed and plaintive than in the noisier foothills. The Great Bear in the sky thrust its muzzle above the sparse treetops to sniff its starry pathway.

The bear left the road at a switchback, picking up a trail that ran westward straight downhill. The air grew warmer as he descended into a gulch with sides so steep and rocky that they had never been logged. He was moving fast, pulled by gravity, when he felt an urge to slow down. A little after he had done so, he became aware of a dark shape on the path in front of him. It was a small rattlesnake, coiled in a strange suspension of consciousness—head resting on its coils, lidless eyes staring stonily into the darkness. It didn't move even when the bear put his nose a few inches away and sniffed. Its stillness made the bear uneasy, and he found the snake's smell unappetizing, so he left it undisturbed and resumed his downhill progress. He enjoyed the swift sensations of movement through the darkness. The white umbels of yarrow plants swam past as though floating free in dark water, and the moonlight was beginning to slant under the treetops, casting long shadows. The bear moved through a world of dark and light stripes. Odd yapping sounds came from the trees on the other side of the gulch.

The sounds were odd because, though something like the barking of a small dog, they lacked the emotional overtones in the sounds made by dogs or other mammals. It wasn't a mammal making them but a spotted owl, so called because its brown plumage was spotted with white. This was a very different bird than the horned owl, shy and rather gentle for an owl, and her appearance contributed to this notion of her character. She was round-headed, plump, and smaller than the horned owl and lacked the ear tufts that make the other bird look so ferocious. Her irises were dark, unlike the glaring yellow irises of the horned owl, and she usually stayed deep in the trees. Although she sounded close by, she was actually calling from the top of the ridge; her cries shared the ventriloquial quality of the crickets.

The calls stopped as the bear reached the bottom of the gulch. There were sandbars in the bed of the nearly dry creek, and he paused to roll in one, finding the sand still warm. Dense thickets of willow and bitter cherry muffled the rocky bed of the creek, and the insinuating trickle of its sluggish flow was almost the only sound except for an occasional mos-

55

quito. As the bear scraped and grunted, life on a smaller scale went on as usual in a dead pine over the sandbar.

An *Euryopis* spider with a metallic shield pattern on the back of his abdomen dragged an ant wrapped in a silken bag past the marshmallow-shaped sporophytes of white pouch fungus that studded the tree from roots to crown. A silverfish looked on nervously as the spider passed, although it needn't have been alarmed, since the spider ate mostly ants. A western pine beetle, the larvae of which were the tree's assassins, peered out from a crevice in the bark. Another *Euryopis* leaped from the trunk of the dead pine and lowered herself quickly to the ground on an invisible strand of silk. On the way she passed a large, reddish brown termite worker which had emerged from the tree: it blundered around for awhile and disappeared back into its colony. These termites belonged to a different species than house-eating termites. They live in standing dead trees and are not much in evidence except in late summer when the young winged queens make their dispersal flights.

A red bat that had finished his feeding for the evening landed with a scratching sound on a fir trunk across the creek and clambered into the foliage, squeaking to himself. The bear turned his head in the direction of the noise. Gray daddy longlegs with orange stripes along their abdomens stalked across the sand beside his rump with impunity, but the brown noctuid moths that filled the warm air had more to fear from him; any that ventured too close were snapped out of the air by jaws capable of pulverizing a cow bone. The moths had a dusty taste though, and the bear went to one of the creek pools to drink. There he caught a brown Pacific tree frog which tasted so interesting that he sat down to see if more might appear.

As he waited, the shimmering tide of moonlight ebbed away up the gulch, and a more substantial darkness arose to replace it. The gulch was so quiet, the sand so warm and soft, that he began to be drowsy. Sighing, he lowered his front end to the sand; he could look for frogs just as well from that position. Then he stretched out his neck so he could scratch his chin on the sand and left his head there instead of raising it again. Now every part of him was pleasantly at rest, except his eyes. The whites glinted in the darkness as he glanced around, but soon it became hard to focus and finally to open them. He was asleep.

The Storm's Edge

The narrow bed of sand, boulders, and willows seemed crowded by the forest that loomed along the gulch. The ponderosa and sugar pines on the northeast wall stretched up bare trunks and gesticulated with spreading branches. The white firs and incense cedars on the shaded southwest wall appeared more static. The dark mass of fir and cedars seemed to rush downward; the pines, to leap up. This illusion of movement reflected the real rise and fall surging calmly and steadily in the trees. Water and nutrients from the rocky soil flowed up the sapwood, and sugar solutions from the green needles circulated through the inner bark. Minute currents of carbon and oxygen molecules eddied and swirled in the branches as the trees breathed. The countless growing tips of the roots stirred silt, sand, and pebbles and pried tiny fragments from the parent rock.

The small bear stirred and opened his eyes for a moment. As the image of stars and treetops formed on his nearsighted retina, he felt a dreamy expansion of his senses so that the mass of trunks and branches overhead seemed a part of his own shaggy hide. The still air pressed against his eardrums with a faint, sweet, ringing sound. These were familiar sensations, however, and he fell asleep again.

The spotted owl flew along the ridgetop until she came to a basin where the ridge merged with another. The basin contained a meadow, but she avoided that, making instead for the dense trees below the rim of the basin. Her methods of hunting were different from those of the horned owl in the foothill pasture. Rather than waiting at the edge of a field or meadow for something to wander into the open, she stayed in the darkness of the forest. There the creatures of darkness on which she preyed—deer mice, flying squirrels, wood rats—felt safe enough to come out where she could catch them. There was also the possibility that a horned owl would prey on her if she ventured into the open.

She landed on a downhill branch of a large white fir, folded her wings, and—becoming quite still—listened. Small rosettes of cloud that had decorated the sunset had been drifting overhead in thicker clumps all evening. At first the moon had modeled icebergs and Himalayas among the dark masses. After it had set, the sky had become a murky pall through which a few glints of starlight shone fitfully. The owl didn't mind this because her eyes were effective in virtually total darkness, and she could hunt by sound. The round, slightly concave face that made her look solemn and benign in the daylight was an effective device for capturing airborne vibrations and funneling them into her ears, which were set at slightly different positions in her skull. This asymmetry gave her an unusual ability to judge how far away a sound was.

It wasn't a very good night for hunting. Capricious winds ruffled the light feathers on the owl's breast and back and rattled the fir branches, obscuring furtive sounds. Low mumbles of thunder came from the south. The owl was hunting farther than ever before from the nesting territory that she and her mate had established, all the available prey nearby already having been gobbled up by their three voracious owlets. The unfamiliar area and threatening weather made her uneasy; she felt an urge to retreat, but her hunting habits proved stronger.

Out in the open meadow, it was only slightly less gloomy. Dry logs and patches of bare soil gleamed if they weren't obscured by the broad leaves of corn lilies. The lilies grew over six feet high and were dense enough to make most of the clearing look more like a canebrake than a mountain meadow. Interspersed with their white-flowered spikes were blooms from plants nearly as tall: larkspur, with deep blue flowers that somehow remained dimly visible in the darkness, and rein orchid, a native orchid with a raceme of small but exquisitely formed greenish blossoms that heavily perfumed the damp air. White violets made an undergrowth to this flower forest, and strange plume moths with narrow, feathery wings fluttered through its glades.

A stiff little breeze ran through the meadow, rattling the lily leaves and riffling the surface of the tiny lake at the south end. It was hardly a lake, really, just a pothole left by an ancient glacier. And it was dying quickly (for a lake), strangled by a quaking bog of rushes and sedges and choked by the clumps of pondweeds and algae that grew richly in its warm, shallow water. Because of its fertility, the lake contained a dense population of animals. Unlike the owl, these creatures seemed indifferent to the ominous sky.

A mob of backswimmers jostled in the black water, feeding on an even denser horde of smaller, mostly microscopic animals. Shiny scavenger beetles covered the muck of the shallow portions, dotted the plant stems, or revolved like tiny space rockets in the constellations of the algae swarms. These were dwarfed by the predacious diving beetles that rowed ponderously through the throng, looking for tadpoles or other big game. Deeper down lurked the real lords of the pool—rough-skinned newts in every developmental stage from pink, gilled larvae to old adults eight inches long with pebbled skins and orange bellies. Spaced every few feet across the bottom, they rested or walked sedately over the ooze as though the Batrachian age of fern forests and endless swamps had never ended. At intervals, one of the adults shot to the surface for a gulp of air, then sank back sluggishly, as though the sudden exertion had stunned it. In the daytime only the largest newts stayed in the open; the rest hid in the pondweed. But the darkness was theirs, and they all came out as if to bask in the weak moonlight that filtered through to the bottom.

A bubble of marsh gas erupted from the ooze and rushed upward in a cloud of silt to break the surface which had just begun to be smooth again. The wind had died briefly, and up in the trees the spotted owl raised her head, appearing longer and thinner as she straightened up. Hearing a deer mouse running over the needles toward its hole at the base of a tree, she launched herself from the branch without hesitation and glided toward the sound. The mouse had paused at the entrance to its nest, so the owl struck with full force and killed quickly, her eyes glaring wide in the darkness. She hardly looked at the mouse until it was dead and still. Pausing a moment to listen, she heard nothing moving except the reawakened wind and flew away with the dangling mouse.

Just as the sky seemed about to clear, there came a distinct roll of thunder and a sound like dry wood creaking and settling. A thin rain began to fall, making popping noises on the pool and alarming the backswimmers on the surface. The deeper creatures remained undisturbed. In the forest the rain only whispered. Carpenter ants continued their attendance on the shiny black aphids they'd domesticated in this locale; the aphids were feeding on the sweet, new branches of white fir. A yearling black-tail buck that had been resting beside the meadow moved deeper into the trees.

The rain dwindled and a few stars reappeared in the west. A gray funnel-weaver spider rushed out of her den, misled by drops of water that fell on the mouth of her web and agitated the strands as if there were something caught there. Finding only droplets, she retreated into her funnel. Her web was near the meadow's edge. Deeper in the big timber, hardly a drop of rain touched the ground. A hairy, red *Geolycosa*, a sedentary relative of the wolf spiders, was able to sit undisturbed at the lip of its vertical burrow on the dusty forest floor.

The mouse paused at the entrance to its nest, so the owl struck with full force, her eyes glaring wide in the darkness.

Then the stars winked out again, and heavy drops began to come down, making thumping sounds on the ground and raising a chaffy smell. But there was still something desultory about the storm here; the rain alternately abated and increased, and the thunder stayed over the horizon. Birds that had been awakened shook themselves and ducked their heads back under their wings. The rain stopped once more, and for a few minutes it was very still, as if the storm was holding its breath and considering where to jump next. Then the sound of a downpour came from the next ridge to the west; the thunder rumbled and a dry wind tossed the treetops around the meadow, knocking down showers of trapped water. The retreating thunder sounded like water rushing away through long, metal pipes.

The spotted owl's fledglings clustered near the broken old incense cedar that held the nest they'd recently left. It did not resemble a nest, being just a clump of mistletoe squashed down flat enough to hold eggs. The owlets were odd-looking creatures. Their bodies had developed the brown and white feathers of the mature owl, but patches of downy nestling plumage remained on their heads here and there, sticking out as though they'd been patched with cotton wool after a brawl. When they moved, the down showed pale against the darkness of the forest floor.

Their behavior wasn't particularly sober. They had outgrown the stage of falling out of trees and could now use their wings for gliding and rudimentary flapping. But they still could not avoid pratfalls, somersaults, and other buffooneries when they tried to pounce on moving objects, although there was little to pounce on except the dead leaves driven past by the fitful storm winds.

When their mother landed on the lowest branch of the nest tree with the deer mouse, the most aggressive of the fledglings forgot flying and used the first method of gaining elevation he'd learned—running up the trunk feet first like a lineman climbs a telephone pole. The old bird had become wary of his importunities though, and when he reached her branch, she fluttered down to the ground and presented another fledgling with the mouse. He gulped it without delay except for the tail, which hung out of the side of his mouth until digestion disconnected it from the rest of the mouse.

The third fledgling had been fed earlier by the male owl, but the aggressive one hadn't eaten that night. This made his play-hunting more intense than that of his siblings. He would probably be the first to go off on his own, perhaps to establish a territory, perhaps to be taken by a horned owl or other predator. He watched the mouse disappear into his brother, then spread his wings and, somewhat to his own surprise, successfully flew twenty feet to a cedar down the side of the gulch. From there the boulders of the creekbed at the bottom were dimly visible.

The Grumbling Stones

A tree frog croaked from a willow thicket, answering the distant thunder. Then a spatter of rain fell and the frog quieted. The young owl gazed in curiosity at the branches from which the pattering and hissing sounds of the rain were coming, feeling an urge to pounce on the sounds. But the pattering stopped and a breeze shook his branch so that he had to shift his weight hastily to stay on. Something fluttered past his tree, moving toward a heavier mass of young trees farther up the gulch. It was the red bat from the bear's sleeping place, disturbed by the rain and seeking better cover.

The bat disappeared and the owl again looked around for an object of interest. He became aware of something moving slowly across the ground and, dropping down to investigate, found himself in possession of a small toad. The toad squeaked in alarm and urinated on the owl's feet, which so surprised the owl that he let go. The toad hopped off a few feet and stopped. The owl, only temporarily disturbed by wet feet and indifferent to any repellent odor (owls seem to have even a worse sense of smell than humans), caught up with it again. After some hesitation—he was still accustomed to having his food presented to him—he ate it.

It hardly rained in the gulch, but thunder and a flood of cold air from the storm woke the young bear. He listened and glanced around without moving until he felt safe, then got up, yawned, and drank at the creek. Tree frogs forgotten, he wandered up the gulch, poking around in the willow thickets but finding little of interest among the paintbrush, columbine, and monkey-flower that grew under the willows. The scarlet blossoms appeared deep black in the diffused starlight.

Here the walls of the gulch constricted, and the creek flowed above ground, rolling small rocks down its bed and making strange echoes against the walls—growls and grumbles that to the small bear sounded uncomfortably like the sounds an angry adult male bear might make. From his experience with the big male that had taken his mother's fancy, there was nothing he was more eager to avoid. Female bears abandon their young after two years in favor of mating, and adult male bears are violently intolerant of young ones.

He left the creek and climbed the west wall of the gulch. When he found a loose rock or log, he would roll it down the slope, partly to see if there was anything to eat underneath, partly to hear the amusing noises it made going downhill. He listened carefully to each rock until it stopped moving, then glanced around furtively in case anything else had heard. But the intermittent dripping of leftover raindrops from the boughs was almost the only other sound; there was nothing to disturb his self-absorption. He stopped to sniff at a tree that a porcupine had recently fed upon; the fermenting sap that oozed from the wounds had an attractively rank smell. The night had entered its most secretive phase.

Even when he had climbed high above the bottom of the gulch, the bear remained in almost as deep a shadow. He was in the wilderness area now, and the forest of white fir and incense cedar hadn't been logged for a long time, if ever. Although a couple of the higher constellations, Draco and Leda, had come out from behind the clouds, very little of their light penetrated the branches of the big trees. Instead of following logging roads, the bear now moved along deer trails which meandered up and down slope, sometimes petering out in landslides and gullies. But he eventually tired of this random progress under the silence of the trees, so he turned and climbed straight upward.

The ridgetop formed a narrow plateau on which the forest was broken by rock formations and grassy glades. In one of these glades a black-tailed jackrabbit drank from a small waterhole, staring wide-eyed at nothing in particular. She stopped drinking when the bear emerged from the trees and, motionless, watched him approach. She didn't have to turn her head to keep him in focus; her eye's spherical lens gave her an extremely wide range of vision. When the bear got too close, she bounced into the willow thicket that bordered the meadow.

The bear wasn't very interested in jackrabbits; they were uncommon in the pine forest and he'd never eaten one, but he idly followed the bobbing, pale shape into the trees. When he came to a black oak that grew beside a grove of cedars, something whizzed over his head. There was a scratching sound on the oak's trunk, and he looked up to see a flying squirrel hanging on the trunk upside-down, scolding him. The scolding was unimpressive—not unlike a Douglas squirrel with a case of laryngitis—and the bear had already been introduced to the flying squirrel's way of investigating intruders into its grove. He still didn't care for it. A flying squirrel's glide is only silent from a distance; it is unnerving to have a rushing noise materialize a few feet above one's head.

The waterhole in the glade had attracted him, so he retraced his steps. He contemplated the mud around the hole which bore the tracks of various animals besides the jackrabbit's—deer, skunks, a porcupine, a weasel—but it seemed too cold for a wallow, although his paws made interesting sucking noises as he pulled them out. He ambled over to a young cedar sapling and stood up with his back against it to scratch.

The scraping of the bear's back against the young tree shook its lower branches violently, disturbing two inhabitants of the tree out of all proportion to the idle pleasure the bear was taking. Among these branches was an extraordinary web, a mass of threads that coalesced subtly into the form of a floating dome. A pair of spiders—called, logically enough, filmy dome spiders—waited under the dome to grab insects that landed on it. They had red legs and black and white abdomens marked with patterns that resembled stylized spiders.

To the filmy dome spiders, the bear's scratching was an earthquake causing shock and emotional dislocation that worked on their limited emotional repertoire to a grisly effect. The pair had been living together amicably since the smaller male had climbed into the web a few days before. This domestic arrangement is traditional for filmy dome spiders and differs from those of the orb weavers, the females of which tolerate the males only for a brief mating period. Upset by the storm of flailing and snapping threads into which her web was suddenly transformed, the female spider pursued and grabbed an object hurrying past her. Of course the object was the male spider running about the web in a panic, but the act of grabbing him triggered an instinctive behavior pattern. She plunged her jaws into his abdomen and injected him with poison, holding him tightly as the web continued to shake.

By the time the bear finished scratching, the male spider was paralyzed, and she had wrapped him in silk from her spinnerets and devoured him. She was hungry after the excitement. Female spiders don't always eat their mates, although this occurs commonly enough to catch the attention of misogynists. The males of many species die soon after mating anyway. In the filmy dome spider's case, however, this cannibalism

The bear wasn't very interested in jackrabbits, but he idly followed the bobbing, pale shape into the trees.

was a biological error. He hadn't mated with her yet. Nevertheless a few hours later the male was nothing but a husk dangling from the bottom of the dome.

As the bear lowered himself back on all fours under the cedar tree, the false dawn was playing its trick, bringing a few drowsy squawks from the forest. The underbrush of raspberry, bedstraw, blueblossom, and golden currant that grew around the glade was noisy with renewed activity after the midnight hiatus. Carpenter ants made a rustling noise of surprising volume as they marched around, and this was punctuated by the squeaks and thumps of meadow mice.

More active than these, although less noisy, was a wandering shrew. This smallest of mammals ran around feverishly slaughtering the bees, flies, and grasshoppers driven down from their perches on the plant stems by the early morning cold. A few minutes after awakening from one of his short naps, the shrew had already filled his stomach but kept up his butchery because the insects were most vulnerable at this time, and he had to lay in a supply for the day. If he was unable to get anything to eat for a few days, he would die of starvation.

As the bear ambled past, the shrew raised his head and peered nearsightedly. When the bear caught the musky shrew odor and lowered his snout to investigate, the small insectivore jumped in alarm, squeaking and pumping his legs in the air; then he sped off and disappeared into the leaf litter. The bear merely snorted—shrews were not good to eat—and went on his way along a trail that led out of the glade into a grove of big firs. From the center of the grove came a piercing shriek, and a dappled fawn jumped up almost under his nose and bounded away. Its cry dwindled in the distance, an eerie sound in the lightless grove.

The bear turned around and returned in haste to the glade. It is surprising how fast bears can move when frightened. When he got into the open, he stopped and looked back over his shoulder; nothing was chasing him. He smelled deer, but then he usually smelled deer. He didn't associate the smell with ear-rending shrieks.

As he stood bemused, two does came out of the trees halfway around the glade and began to move in his direction. This was unusual. Deer usually stared a moment, then began to edge away. They had never stared at him with the strange fixity that these two displayed. There was a stiffness about their gait that made him uneasy.

When they had come abreast of him, one of the deer stopped and began to scold the bear, a sound somewhere between the chucking of a squirrel and the yowling of an alley cat. The other kept moving in a curve that would have carried her out of his sight. The bear began to back up and then caught a flash of movement in the corner of his eye as the silent deer rushed him.

He reached a big sugar pine just ahead of her and climbed twenty feet before he looked back. They were both at the bottom watching him. They would not have done this to a full-grown bear, of course, even if he had eaten their fawn; but a half-grown one or a bobcat or coyote had to watch out for the unpredictable deer, especially does with fawns or bucks in rut. Treeing him seemed to satisfy them; they moved off across the clearing and started grazing. The bear stayed in the tree. He snapped at a large noctuid moth that flew past his nose. The moth flew on unscathed.

The Persistent Fabric

Alarmed by the clash of the bear's jaws, the furry-bodied noctuid moth veered off across the glade. He had been following the pheromone scent of a female moth, but now he was confused. He fluttered around at random until a tympanic membrane (the same kind of membrane as the human eardrum) on the left side of his thorax began to vibrate. This vibration made him turn to the right, away from its cause. The membrane was sensitive to vibrations of high frequency, and it was vibrating to the

69

echolocation cries of the red bat that earlier had crawled into the tree at the bottom of the gulch. The cries warned the moth that a potential enemy was near.

But the bat had already heard the echoes of his cries from the moth's body. When the echoes began to fade after the moth turned, he knew his prey was retreating and flew faster. As the bat began to overtake him, the membranes on both sides of the moth's body vibrated harder, and the insect began to fly erratically. The bat countered this by speeding up his cries so that, as a filmed motion is made to seem smoother by speeding up a movie camera and shooting more frames, he got a clearer notion of the moth's movements.

When the bat was right behind him, the moth folded his wings and dropped toward the ground. The bat swooped quickly and caught him by the abdomen. The moth fluttered violently, but the bat clamped the insect firmly against his pelvis and bit off thorax and abdomen, letting the head and wings fall. The intricately scaled, brown wings drifted down like dry leaves to land silently in the grass.

The bear yawned and shifted his position on the branch. The moth's last moments had been an obscure flickering in the darkness to him. He felt that it would be light soon. When it was warm, it would be pleasant to wallow in the mud of the sink hole. He heard the deer moving around in the grass and felt a pang of anxiety, but a moment later his unconscious confidence had returned. The idea that his life could be permanently disrupted, could end, was unknown to him; so he was patient. He rubbed his gums on the bark of the tree and waited for the deer to go away.

In the canyon west of the glade, a pair of pygmy owls began to call back and forth. Like the burrowing owl in the pasture, they were birds of the dawn. Scaled to match the chickadees and juncos they preyed upon, these little owls had a soprano call like children singing one note over and over. They had not been singing for long before the grass and the trees around the glade turned a uniform pale blue, as if cut from the same piece of cerulean satin.

As the stars faded a gray, crested wood pewee woke up and began his song, a series of buzzing notes that might have come from a grasshopper. Although it wasn't the most musical of the songs that greeted the light, it was almost always the first. A robin called next, and soon the whole range of small forest birds began their songs and calls, without which the daytime would be a drab affair.

Sunlight warmed the air above the trees, driving a breeze through the branches and making them heave and sigh. The bear rode up and down on his perch, and the deer across the pasture pricked up their ears at the wind sounds. As the sunlight climbed down from the treetops, throwing orange patches on the blue grass, the deer edged into the shadow of the trees until all at once it seemed that they had disappeared. The light reached the lower branches of the cedar against which the bear had scratched himself, illuminating a strand of silk running from the filmy dome web to the branch above. A male filmy dome spider descended this strand and reached out to pluck at the web, announcing his presence to the still-unmated female.

The sun rose above the top of the ravine. Soil and branches touched by the slanting rays turned scarlet for a moment.

PART THREE
The Foxtail Pine

The Foxtail Pine

The very silence has another quality than the silence of the day.
And it is full of half-heard whispers—whispers that
startle—the ghosts of sounds long dead.
Ambrose Bierce, "A Tough Tussle"

FROM THE CANADIAN ZONE LAKE, the valley, foothills, and ponderosa pine forest seemed insignificant interruptions in a world of peaks. The North Yolla Bollys and Trinity Alps lay to the north; the Sierra-Cascades marched along the entire eastern horizon; and the views south and west were blocked by the South Yolla Bolly peaks which stood directly overhead. The lake matched the unassuming scale of the gentle summits it mirrored. Only a hundred feet or so across, it was a perfect glacial tarn in miniature, carved out at the base of a rocky cirque and neatly dammed by a moraine that was too innocent of topsoil to have much growing on it except lupines.

The stream that fed the lake splashed down from the snow of the peaks, then ran through a sloping delta covered with rushes and sedges before entering the lake. Much of the lake was shallow, filled with quantities of silt scraped from the rocks by the stream over the years, but a deep place still remained on the side away from the stream entrance. The water left the lake through a channel on one side of the moraine and flowed quickly past a row of undersized lodgepole pines that grew on the thin, waterlogged soil.

75

Bigger lodgepoles stood in pockets of deeper soil among the tumbled boulder piles on the other two sides of the lake along with a few giant ponderosa pines on warm, dry spots. But the loose, golden bark and pliant needles of the ponderosas looked out of place in this region of bare rock and subarctic winters. The smooth, silver bark and stiff, viridian needles of the lodgepoles fitted in better. Past the boulder piles, areas that had not been scraped bare of topsoil by the glacier were covered with stands of red fir—massive, colorful trees with dark purple bark and blue green foliage. White fir, another straggler from the ponderosa pine forest, grew in favorable locations, but the incense cedar had been left behind.

The lakesides had not been free of snow for very long, and flowers that had faded from the foothills in April and from the ponderosa forest in June—shooting stars, forget-me-nots, and buttercups—were in blossom here. The corn lilies were still in the bud. A fine lawn of clover (left over perhaps from the days when the lake was a summer sheep pasture) embroidered with yellow cinquefoil and anemones ran down to the water. The lupine was in blossom too, its purple flowers making the moraine appear incandescent in the warm, late-afternoon light. Even the shady spots under the cliffs and boulders held clumps of bright magenta penstemon and sulfur-flowered eriogonum. Some plants that were in flower in the ponderosa pine forest, such as pennyroyal, whitethorn, and yarrow, also bloomed beside the lake now.

Many other reproductive activities that had run their course at lower altitudes were still in full swing around the lake. Birds sat on eggs; some mammals had just given birth; and the gravel of the stream sheltered the year's crop of trout fry. The waters of the lake itself swarmed with activity that made the foothill creekbeds seem sluggish by comparison. But behind this liveliness was an urgency which the foothill creatures could not know. In a few months most of the birds would fly away, most of the mammals would disappear beneath the snow, and the creatures of the lake would lie dormant under the mud. Even the hardy trout would move only when necessary in order to conserve the dwindling supply of dissolved oxygen under a ceiling of ice.

The Sinking Horde

Hemmed in by the peaks, the lake lost the sun early. As the yellow rays faded, its surface changed from blue to green and pink—the colors of the still sunlit rocks and trees. Hundreds of spreading circles disturbed the surface as trout rose to feed on the delicate mayflies laying their eggs in the water. Among the treetops where sunbeams persisted, gnat swarms eddied like thickly falling snow against the dark branches of fir and pine.

The daytime animals hurried to fill their stomachs. A robin flew across the lake, heading for the clover, and a small flock of swallows skimmed over the water. A little sharp-shinned hawk that had a nest somewhere on the south slope of the peaks swooped over the ridgetop, trying to drive small birds out of the bushes; she stilled against the wind for a moment, then slipped out of sight.

A hermit thrush sang in a white fir grove below the lake, its exquisite phrases virtually the only sounds in the grove. The song tumbled from the small, brown bird's throat, descended the columns of the trunks, filtered through the dark branches, and faded gravely into the blue haze of the encroaching darkness. The trees themselves seemed rapt as if their stillness was more than vegetative, concealing some sympathetic vibration of the inner bark.

Under the trees a jumping spider made his last capture of the day. His tan and gray body perfectly matched the bark chips and pebbles around him as he crouched motionless a few inches from a fat, black fly for several moments before he pounced. He caught it with a single bound of about ten times his own length, holding it tight until his poison began to work. Then he turned the fly belly up and fed. His meal was made less than dignified by the necessity of dodging a passing column of carpenter ants. Afterwards he crawled under a piece of bark to spend the night in a silk-lined nest, safe from prowling wolf spiders.

As the sunlight receded up the cliffs, the trout strikes on the lake tapered off, replaced by the smaller but infinitely more numerous rings made by the huge backswimmer population as they took their turn at the mayflies. Occasionally, one of these upside-down-swimming water bugs would rise to the surface and flip itself right side up, thus revealing its handsome black- and orange-striped abdomen and jade green head. It would lie still, jostled by its upside-down compatriots (some of whom might occasionally attack its underside) until its back had dried. Then it would open hidden wings and, ascending in a wide arc, disappear into the fading sky. Most of these flyers merely landed on the other side of the lake, but a few managed to disperse to other bodies of water; these usually turned out to be as crowded with backswimmers as the one the emigrant had just left.

A band-winged grasshopper flashed her bright yellow orange wings across the clover and landed in the water, where she was immediately attacked by the local backswimmers. She kicked out and drove them away, but she had been stung twice almost immediately and knocked on her side so that her wings were wet and useless. Backswimmer stings are not much less painful than bee stings, and even the lake's trout generally left them alone, though a larger fish might swallow one from time to time after mouthing and dropping it repeatedly as if it were hot.

The voracious bugs didn't often seem to catch the mayflies at which they lunged, but they may have been more successful with the many smaller creatures active on the surface. Although the number of backswimmers was great enough to entirely cover the mud of the shallower parts, they were far from being the most numerous organisms in the lake.

If fallen grasshoppers and mayfly eggs were unavailable, they could always subsist on the nekton—the clouds of tiny, self-propelled organisms that the lake supported. Microscopic crustaceans and red water mites jigged through the open water, while roundworms, rotifers (which look like tiny carpet sweepers), protozoans, and many kinds of insect larvae thronged the plants and mud.

As the light faded, the algae upon which nekton feed—green desmids, golden glassy diatoms, whip-tailed euglenoids, and globular volvocines—began to sink as their photosynthetic activity slowed. The tiny animals sank with them, and the rings on the surface diminished as the back-swimmers followed. When the last smear of sunlight left the top of the cliffs, the lake was a mirror, slightly flyspecked but smooth as glass.

A spotted sandpiper landed on the gravel beach where the stream entered the lake. As she touched her feet to the ground, she whistled—a sad sound to human ears, like the cries of other shorebirds. But she had nothing in particular to be sad about. She had mated this year and, a few days earlier, had laid four green eggs in a grass-lined hollow on the sloping ground between the water and the cliff. Her mate was there sitting on them.

After eating a wolf spider that had just come out into the open, the robin-sized sandpiper whistled again and flew off to another little beach partway around the lake. Her way of flying was a little unusual; although there was nothing to stop her from making a beeline to her destination, she approached it instead by a semicircular flight that took her over the middle of the lake. Landing again she ran back and forth, pausing every few seconds to bob her tail up and down, and ate a leafhopper and two ants. Then she made another semicircular flight to an unexplored part of the first beach. In the dusk her fluttering seemed like a bat's flight more than a bird's, but this illusion was dispelled when she flashed her white underside on landing.

While it might seem an unnecessary expenditure of energy, this round-about way of flying suited the sandpiper's way of perceiving the world. An owl flies straight because it sees through the long, narrow cone of binocular vision; but the sandpiper's eyes were on the sides of her head, rather than in front. Instead of looking across the lake, one might say that she looked around it; she could see most of the shoreline without turning her head. This wide angle of vision combined with the openness of the shoreline to give her optimum use of the available light. She could stay active later than other birds, hunting the creeping things that hid from the sunlight.

She found a purplish sac spider that had just emerged from its woven retreat under a log beside the beach and speared it with her beak after bobbing up and down over it a few times. Her roundabout vision didn't give her much depth perception, but she could judge distance by chang-ing the angle from which she looked at an object, thus the bobbing. Otherwise she had little need for straightness in a world full of circular shapes: eggs, pebbles, lakes, the curve of the horizon (seen with sand-piper eyes), the ovals of migration flyways.

She stayed on the shore until the darkness hid the leopard-spot clouds that had begun to drift over and the moon teetered on the clifftop like a crooked smile. The lake became a black well, and the big brown bats from the cliffs came down to flap and squeak across it, taking their turn at the mayflies. The grassy shoreline seemed to contract around the wa-ter, and the lone bird's whistles sounded disembodied in the gloom.

The Rippling Mountain

In the lakeside grass thousands of dwarf spiders, like tiny black or brown beads, ran around or sat in sheet webs stretched among the stems. Other thousands of equally tiny orb weavers that had waited until the birds were asleep now began to spin their half-dollar webs among the needles of pine and fir. Among the smallest of invertebrate predators, these were also among the most important, if only because they, like the diminutive moths, flies, and bugs on which they preyed, were so numerous. The quantity of brown fir and pine needles eaten hollow by needle-miner larvae testified to the numbers of this tiny species. Some trees were entirely brown at the top, though the drying winds of winter had probably contributed to this effect too.

Even as the spiders spun their webs, drops of dew formed on the strands. The moisture that the sun had evaporated from the lake during the day was already condensing on every available surface as the temperature fell rapidly. The grass was drenched, and the clover leaves—closed now in the darkness—hung heavy with the droplets that clung to their hairy stems. The rocks above, though, were still warm and dry, radiating stored heat from the sun.

Among these rocks foraged one of the least numerous of predators—a pine marten. He was about the size of a cat, though longer and lower to the ground, with rounded ears, bright black eyes, and brown fur except for an orange chest patch. He was in thin summer pelage so his fur looked a little scruffy. But there was nothing awkward about him. Like other members of the weasel family, he moved so sinuously that he seemed almost free of gravity, as though his movements depended no more on the pressure of foot to ground than does the windblown drifting of fallen leaves. And his movements, seldom random, made less noise than falling leaves; there was something to see or smell at every turn or lift of his head. His smallest motion displayed the energy and concentration that a human dancer or athlete can maintain for a couple of hours, but the marten was like this most of the time he was awake.

Placing his forepaws on a tree trunk, the marten reached up to pluck one of the black and bronze cicadas, patterned like antique, lacquered helmets, that had sung through the hot afternoon. Without a pause, he jumped down and moved off swiftly, crunching the insect between his jaws. He could always fill his stomach in the summer, but in the winter it was not so easy. Then martens go down to the ponderosa pine forest where the snow is less deep and there are small birds and Douglas squirrels to catch in the trees. But when the thaw comes, they always climb back to the high, rocky places, attracted—like the sandpiper and other migratory birds—by the abundant life that emerges from under the snow and ice.

He was looking for wood rat signs—not the dusky-footed wood rats of the foothills, but an alpine species called bushy-tailed wood rats because their tails are densely furred and horizontally flattened like a squirrel's. In the absence of the rabbitlike pikas, whose range in the Klamath Mountains doesn't start until farther north, they were a favored prey, being easier to catch than chipmunks or ground squirrels. They didn't live down long, narrow tunnels but in more accessible caves and rock crevices. But they were also harder to find, so the marten had to cover large areas.

He didn't find anything around the lake so he climbed away from it over a boulder-strewn buttress that ran down from the peaks. On the other side stretched a long meadow lined with big red firs in which a small flock of dusky grouse had taken refuge. The birds had made a great deal of noise as they climbed the trees by flying from branch to branch, but they had settled down to sleep and were quiet now. Meadows didn't usually interest the marten, however, because their dense herbage impeded his movements, and he didn't descend into this one.

He kept on along the buttress until the boulders and tree-grown patches of soil gave way to steep slopes of decayed rock. At the bottom of these stood piles of scree—fragments that had cracked off the rock formations farther up and slid to the bottom. The marten sniffed around these piles with care but again found nothing, so he started up the slope.

The protruding rock from which the scree had broken was a soft red schist, so lichen crusted and eroded that it resembled dry bone cracked and exposed until the crumbled surface of the marrow was revealed.

Despite the apparent barrenness, each crevice and depression on the slopes was spun over with spider webs, and this looked very strange. As the pale webs moved in the breeze and light from the sinking moon gleamed on the fluttering sheets of silk, the whole mountainside seemed alive with a scaly movement, quite silent and unearthly. It was difficult to see what the spiders lived on, although comatose deer flies and bumblebees clung to sparse bunch grasses and lupines.

The marten zigzagged up the slope, tracing thin threads and tangles of scent until he emerged onto a platform of bare rock interspersed with dwarfed lodgepole and foxtail pines. It was the top of the South Yolla Bolly range, and he smelled snow. The snowfields and the pale rocks surrounding them were a deep green in the moonlight. Along with the scent of the snow, the breeze carried something he found more interesting. It was barely a smell, rather an insinuation of warm-blooded staleness among the dusty purity of weathered minerals. He had to cast around for a time before he located its source—a rock outcropping with a brushy depression at one end.

He bounded without hesitation into the darkness of a cleft in the exposed rock, nose twitching and ears cocked for the sounds of panic from further inside. But there were none. In the sheltered hollow formed by the cleft, he found only dust and dry twigs. It was empty. A few minutes spent sniffing around for an escape hole yielded no results, so he came out again. On the way, he stopped to sniff at a decayed pile of fecal pellets and a deposit of dried urine so thick and hard it was like a dark brown mineral—the product of hundreds of wood rat generations that had lived in the cleft. Good nest sites being scarce, rats would live there again, but the most recent inhabitants had been removed by a weasel in June.

83

The marten zigzagged up the slope, tracing tangles of scent until he emerged onto a platform of bare rock interspersed with dwarfed lodgepole and foxtail pines.

A strange noise was moving across the expanse of snow and scree and twisted pine when the marten reemerged. It sounded close by at one moment, then far away—a booming sound like a winter avalanche. It made him uneasy, so he turned to go back the way he had come. The sound was produced by powerful eddies of wind rushing through the trees and causing their branches to roar and snap. The wind eddies left wakes of tossing branches behind them as might an animal moving in brush. In the moonlight it looked as if heavy but invisible animals were running through the stunted pines. Clouds of dust and twigs were lifted and swirled high into the darkness with dizzying speed.

The top of the range was a harsh place. Normally, the stars shone with painful intensity, and meteors streaked overhead as though the galaxy meant to explode and rain stars. The Big Dipper rode high, and Scorpio was usually visible, crawling along the southern horizon with the red star of its stinger curled over its back. But tonight the sky to the south was increasingly obscured by a layer of clouds that swiftly encroached on the moon and were flushed deep purple with sporadic lightning.

The marten explored his way back down the ridge, boldly intruding into anything that interested him. Martens are so free of caution that they can be caught in the same live trap several times over a short period of time. Like the bear that was at that moment eating lily bulbs in the ponderosa forest, it was the marten's second summer in the world. He had seen more of it than the bear, having been born near the south fork of the Trinity River, some fifty miles to the northwest. He'd reached the Yolla Bollys a month earlier, after a winter of wanderings that had twice been hastened by meetings with other martens. Like other members of the weasel family, the marten is an unsociable animal.

Now he had lived through his first winter and reached an area where populations of his species were sparse and uncompetitive, this being near the southern limit of marten range. He was likely to be a survivor. But such security caused no relaxation on his part. Aside from the fact that relaxation is not in the nature of martens, he'd just become sexually mature. In the past month his testicles had grown from pea to hazelnut size, and they wouldn't shrink back again for another month. All he could do in the meantime was rub himself against branches. There weren't any females nearby, and it probably wouldn't have helped if there were. Male martens don't often mate successfully their first season.

The Trickster

The long meadow that the marten had passed earlier appeared empty in the moonlight, but faint sounds came from the deep trenches of shadow cast by the trees along its edge—a hesitant rustle, a long silence, then delicate crunchings. One of the deer spending the summer around the meadow was sampling the sweet top of a corn lily. There were five deer: two yearling does, an older doe with a fawn, and a two-point buck, his antlers in velvet. The buck was eating grass a little distance from the does, and he seemed uncomfortable; he kept shaking his head and twitching his ears. Perhaps he had a case of mites.

The deer were aware of three basic smells in the meadow: the strong, boggy smell of the meadow itself; the dry, resinous smell from trees and boulder piles; and the faint but rank smell of ferns, nettles, and rotting wood from the ravine at the top of the meadow. When deer smell something strange, they can determine its general location by the background odors that come with it. A current of cold, acrid air blowing down the meadow made the older doe raise her head abruptly, ears turned toward the ravine. There was no sound, but she snorted and hurried toward the trees in the other direction, the fawn behind her.

The others had raised their heads too, but not hearing or smelling anything unusual, stood still for a moment. Pieces of rush hanging out of the buck's mouth gave him a bovine aspect, like a steer eating hay.

Then the loud report of a large branch breaking echoed from the ravine. The other deer followed the doe into the trees with the camellike gait deer adopt when they feel intruded upon and move prudently but unwillingly toward cover.

Quite suddenly a large bear emerged from the shadows that the deer had just vacated. He had come down from the ravine silently after an impatient encounter with a fallen tree. He was following a path made and used mostly by bears. It didn't wander like deer paths, but led purposefully to the bottom of the meadow, through another little ravine, then across a clearing, which could hardly be called a meadow since its soil was only thinly covered with lupines and bunch grass. The stream from the lake's overflow had cut a deep, alder-bordered bed through the clearing, and it rushed past without watering the soil. Perhaps it had been a meadow before soil erosion from overgrazing in the nineteenth century caused the stream to cut the deep channel.

A long-legged coyote had been standing quietly at the lower end of this barren clearing for fifteen minutes, waiting for a gopher to come out of its hole. The gophers preferred the bare clearing to the lush meadow upstream because the soil here was much better drained, and they weren't continually flooded out of their homes. As a result the clearing teemed with them. They virtually plowed it every year with their tunneling.

But they were hard to catch above ground. The coyote had almost given up when his practiced eye caught a movement in the darkness of the hole. He immediately reared back on his hind legs and, as the rodent's beady eyes appeared in the moonlight, brought both forepaws down hard. He darted his snout in to grab the stunned gopher before it fell back down the hole and lifted it into the air with a flip of his head.

The bear arrived at the upper edge of the clearing just as the coyote started his spring. He stopped and watched the whole performance with great attention. When the gopher appeared, dangling from the coyote's jaws, the bear's expression changed. His eyes widened and the muscles of his neck and jaws tightened with desire. He moved toward the coyote who was indulging in the same little head-tossing dance of triumph as a dog might who has just retrieved a stick. The coyote didn't hear his rival until he was halfway across the clearing. When he finally looked around, the bear broke into a gallop, sounding rather like a horse on the beaten earth of the path. He was no match for the coyote, however, who streaked off soundlessly toward the trees.

The bear hurried to the gopher's hole, but the coyote had taken his catch with him instead of dropping it in his surprise. Convinced of this, the bear forgot the entire affair and moved along. The coyote turned half around at the edge of the trees and, seeing the bear stop to sniff the gopher hole, also relaxed and disappeared into the shadows at a trot. The clearing was still for a few minutes. Then a series of yaps merging into a wail rose from the trees. Whether it was to mock the bear or alert other coyotes or accomplish some other purpose, only the wailer knew.

The Uneasy Silence

The coyote snapped up the gopher, perhaps to be regurgitated later to feed pups, and quickly departed the stand of mature red fir that surrounded the dry clearing. After he had drifted away, the forest lapsed into a hush that was different from the quietness of meadows and lakesides. There the stillness was enlivened by the sounds of moving water or wind, but very little of this penetrated far into the trees. The thick screen of needles and branches was a very effective sound insulator.

The screen also kept out much of the light that fell on the open places. One could stand in some parts of the grove and not see a single star. Even the moonlight came through only in patches, and it seemed abnormally bright in the darkness. Sometimes when light fell on the quartz veins in rock outcroppings, the patches appeared to be solid, to glow from within. Sunlight was shaded out almost as effectively as moonlight, and hardly anything except fungus grew on the dense brown mat of needles. The rocks were quite free of moss and lichen.

Intense as it was, the silence under the big firs was not particularly tranquil. At intervals there were faint but sharp rustling and snapping sounds. Red fir wood is brittle and breaks easily; the ground was littered with twigs and branches that had snapped off from their own weight. Like the patches of moonlight, these sounds were enhanced by the obscurity of their surroundings. They seemed eerie and portentous.

Through this uneasy silence crept a large black millipede, handsomely decorated with red gold stripes along his shiny sides. He moved slowly as though sluggish from the cold, but actually the evening drop in temperature had stimulated him—he'd spent the sunlight hours curled under a rock. As he undulated along, the millipede rotated his short antennae to test the ground for a sweetness of plant decay richer than that of the dry needles and twigs.

He bumped into the fungus-covered base of a twenty-foot snag—all that remained of a long-dead red fir. It was set a little apart from the other trees. After stopping for a little while as if to muse on this new development, he crawled around the base until he came to a place where the bark had fallen off and revealed excavations made by generations of wood-eating creatures. One hole near the bottom tasted of termites. This attracted him and he climbed into it, pushing his way past the spongy sides with approximately two hundred powerful legs.

He found the absolute darkness inside comfortable; in a little while the passage opened up, and he didn't have to squeeze to get through. Something touched the sensitive spots along his sides, and the millipede stopped again, ready to curl up in defense. But the camel cricket that had touched him with its sensitive antennae found the myriapod distasteful and quickly drew back. Glands full of a noxious substance dotted the millipede's calcareous hide, providing an effective defense. The cricket, a small fungus-colored insect with exceptionally long antennae, backed into a side gallery. The millipede moved deeper into the snag, passing herds of wood lice grazing on the fungus filaments that riddled the dead wood. Shiny dysderid spiders with beetlelike abdomens and jaws especially adapted for cracking wood louse shells lurked in the tunnels, but they didn't bother him. He kept going until he reached the termite nest where he stayed to scavenge the half-chewed wood and other garbage that lay in unused chambers.

The gallery into which the camel cricket retreated from the millipede would have revealed, if illuminated, a lovely range of colors in its vaultings, arches, and pillars of decayed wood—from lemon yellow to rust and coral, with unexpected touches of emerald and Prussian blue. The colors originated from the subtle chemistries of darkness, though, and would have faded to dull beige in sunlight. The cricket followed the gallery to its end at an old woodpecker hole and, crawling to the edge, waved her antennae in the open air. Outside, the moon had set on the lower part of the grove, but the upper boughs were still sprinkled with light.

A dark shape passed swiftly across the moonlit background. The cricket's antennae were agitated by a puff of displaced air as a flying squirrel glided in to land beside the woodpecker hole. She was a silky furred animal, gray on top and white below, with a rufous fringe covering the loose membranes of skin between fore and back paws. Her eyes, large even for a nocturnal animal, caught the wispy movement of the cricket's antennae, and she reached around and plucked the insect out of the hole. Holding it in her mouth like a nut, she climbed to a bigger hole and disappeared.

The five blind infants to which she had given birth a few days previously attacked her teats as soon as they heard her land on the bark-lined nest at the bottom of the hole. They couldn't hold up their heads without trembling, but they were insistent. After eating the cricket, she settled down to nurse, her eyes half shut. The muffled squeals and sucking noises of the babies echoed a little way into the dark galleries around the nest, but the rotten wood was like cork insulation, and the sounds didn't carry very far.

The forest around the snag hadn't been so quiet during the winter and spring. Three male squirrels and another female had shared the nest with her then. The five had spent the cold winter days curled together in a tight ball of fur and the nights foraging or playing complicated sexual games of tag. She had been the first to become pregnant and her disposition had changed after that. She had turned on the other female and eventually driven her away, then dealt with each of the males in the same manner until she was alone in the snag.

It was a perfect nest for flying squirrels. Because no boughs connected the snag with other trees, the Douglas squirrels didn't want it. They couldn't jump far enough to reach it and wouldn't use a nest that could only be reached over the ground. If they had been able to use it, they would invariably have driven the flying squirrels away, being larger and more aggressive. The snag also provided a good defense against predators; a marten or weasel climbing it would have to turn around and climb down again to chase an escaping flying squirrel. There was only room in this perfect site for one nest and, after winning her monopoly, the squirrel guarded it jealously.

After the babies had gone back to sleep and she had taken a short nap, she looked out again. The moon was down and a few stars showed in the northeast; otherwise the trees lifted their tops toward an absolute murk. Anticipatory thunder grumbled to the south. But she was hungry most of the time now, so she went out to forage again.

The first glide took her sixty feet to a tree where she kept an emergency nest. She usually went to this tree first and paused a moment to see if some enemy had been waiting for her to come out. Then she continued on in a westward direction. On the other side of the forest from the dry meadow was a deep ravine containing a skinny and very shallow lake. The slopes of this ravine were good places to find the fungi she liked to eat. Like the wood rat, she followed habitual pathways. If one of the trees on which she was accustomed to land had been cut down, she would have kept trying to land on it and suffered unpleasant surprises several times before she accepted its absence.

At the ravine she saw a puffball on the ground and glided down toward it, braking with her tail just before landing. Her tail was flatter than those of other squirrels and made a good rudder—she could turn in mid-air with it. The puffball was old and dry, however, so she dropped it. A deer mouse that had been cutting grass stems nearby ran past her and disappeared into a hole at the base of a tree. The squirrel sniffed at the edges of the mouse hole with interest; she was only an incidental predator, but she liked meat. This wasn't very promising though, so she moved off still sniffing at the ground. She was looking for truffles, tasty fungi which she could smell underneath the fir needles and soil that hid them from sight.

The Storm's Center

The storm hit the fir forest almost without warning. The branches had obscured the faraway thunder and lightning, and the peaks had screened the southern sky from which the storm was approaching. So it was deceptively quiet until the lightning jumped the peaks; then the night was cracked down the middle by a thick violet bolt of it. The peal that accompanied the lightning shook the ground.

There was a moment of shocked silence; then a whispering sound began somewhere on the higher slopes, growing steadily louder as it approached. Branches began to jump and creak, and there were rattling

92

The cricket's antennae were agitated by a puff of displaced air as a flying squirrel glided in to land beside the woodpecker hole.

noises against the trunks of the big trees. It was hail. As its full force hit the forest, the whisper rose to a roar, and the rattling accelerated to an ominous tattoo, like drums before an execution.

The hailstones were marble sized and came down with the force of spent bullets, knocking birds off their perches and bouncing crazily against branches and ground. The birds were in a bad way. The lightning blinded them and they fluttered around in panic, breaking their fragile bones against the trunks. Some found new perches and some made their way to the temporary safety of the ground.

In the ravine beside the narrow lake, the hailstones tore apart the nest of a pair of Lincoln's sparrows. The trout fled into the deepest parts of the lake to escape the hail, which sounded even more awesome under-water where a deep reverberation added to the roaring and rattling. The stones skipped and splashed on the surface, turning it into a stormy sea for the backswimmers. They darted back and forth, trying to dodge the individual stones as they hit.

After the first few peals, the thunder seemed not so much heard as felt —a disturbance in the bone marrow more than the ears. The infant flying squirrels awoke in terror. For all they knew, the strange violence was in the nest with them. Scarlet light flashed behind their closed eyelids, and a hailstone bounced into the hole and landed on them. They fought to get away from the burning thing.

Much of the forest floor was protected by the dense canopy of branches above, but on the side of the ravine where the trees grew more sparsely, the adult flying squirrel got the full force of the hail. It knocked her several feet down the slope before she could reach shelter. When she recovered from this shock, she climbed the nearest tree and tried to see her way back to the nest. She was off her usual route, and there was nothing to see except the leaden sheets of falling hail and the greater darkness of the ravine. She was so frightened that she launched herself into the air anyway, heading away from the ravine; halfway through her glide, a wind-driven barrage of hail threw her back to the ground.

When she recovered and looked up, she saw four balls of green fire a few feet from her nose—the reflection of lightning in the eyes of the doe and fawn. The doe jumped to her feet and the squirrel went up a tree. She crawled out on an upper branch and crouched with her tail over her back and her eyes half-closed. By this time, she was in a mild state of shock, her heart beating fast and her legs heavy and weak. She no longer wanted to go anywhere, only to cling to the branch.

In ten minutes the hail stopped as suddenly as it had begun. The lightning split the darkness in a final attempt to blow the night to pieces, then leapt away northward. The wind that swept through in its wake shattered the clots of hail on some of the branches, and the fragments fell with tinkling sounds.

The squirrel flicked her tail and began to look around. Her stomach felt painfully empty, so when she saw a pale shape on the ground on her way back to the nest, she glided down to investigate. It was an olive-sided flycatcher fledgling, its neck broken by the storm. The squirrel bit through the pale feathers and devoured the still warm breast muscles. After that she felt tired but thirsty, so she visited the stream at the other side of her grove. When she finally returned to the nest, the young squirrels wouldn't let her rest until she had fed them again.

After the wind had blown down the last of the hail fragments, something continued to fall—soft objects that thudded faintly on the ground instead of tinkling. They bounced as they landed, lay curled up quietly for a moment, then crawled for the nearest tree. They were caterpillars: green loopers and brown, hammer-headed budworms. Although the storm had knocked many of them down, they had been falling in fair numbers before it started. The rain of caterpillars went on at a fairly steady rate on some nights of this season.

The odd thing about this phenomenon was that it seemed to occur in a vacuum. No horde of beetles chased the loopers and budworms from the branches, but they kept dropping off anyway, either because other caterpillars touched them or because the branches shook in a breeze. Nor did more than an occasional predator take advantage of them on the ground. But this strange dripping of bodies continued, apparently to nobody's benefit, least of all their own.

There are more of such gaps in the fabric of life here than in the foothills or the ponderosa pines, more places where only a few kinds of animals, or no animals at all, are active. Fewer species are adapted to a habitat that is covered with five or more feet of snow for half the year. The caterpillars might all die from weather or disease, but their parent moths will soon reinvade, attracted by the unvaried but constant supply of conifer needles. It is more difficult for predators such as ground beetles to benefit from an abundance of caterpillars, because that abundance is too transient and unstable. So there were fewer ground beetles here and more caterpillars.

This reduced diversity made the hiatus that occurred toward the end of the night even longer and quieter than in the chaparral or the incense cedars. Still another factor was the bone-chilling cold, which congealed time into a heavy, dense medium in which—like water that hovers near the freezing point—life becomes sluggish. Even owls were seldom heard unless some northern species wandered down in winter. Poor-wills called from the meadows now and again, their voices sounding even more lost and tremulous than at lower altitudes.

The lakes and meadows stored some of the day's heat so they remained livelier than the forest or the bare slopes. In the ravine the rainbow trout had come out of their storm cellars among the reeds and clumps of green algae. The algae were buoyed up by softball-sized bubbles of marsh gas, causing the lake bottom to resemble the extraterrestrial landscapes on the jackets of science fiction books. The trout lined up at the stream mouth to bathe their gills in the freshly oxygenated water tumbling over the pebbles. They kept an eye on the dim curve of the lake's surface, and any movement above it sent them back into the depths. They had reflective eyes which gleamed pale red in a flashlight beam.

In the reedy shallows at the other end of the lake, where the water stayed warmer, the backswimmers kept up their perpetual revolutions. Their buoyancy forced them toward the surface if they lay quiet, so each bug performed an erratic dance to stay down—a jerk forward, a suspended moment, then slow rising and another forward jerk. Some clung to the mud of the bottom. Beyond the reeds, the lake narrowed to a channel populated by scavenger beetles and striders; then it emptied abruptly down a steep jumble of boulders and bare soil as the ravine ended in midair.

It was a hanging ravine, truncated by a much broader, deeper gouge in the mountainside that seemed, from the steepness and bareness of its sides, to have been recently caused. In fact it was the track of the long-vanished glacier, kept fresh by recurring slides and avalanches on its unstable slopes. The sudden drop was like a trap door opening out of the dense forest. The northern sky appeared, brilliant above the pale clouds of the receding storm. The stars looked hard as metal from this door, but the thin dots and dashes of yellow light from the pitch black valley wavered spectrally and even disappeared entirely from time to time. The sound of running water came from the gorge, but no bottom to it was visible in the starlight.

When the night had been absolutely still for so long that it seemed nothing would ever happen again, a moving shadow appeared suddenly among the boulders of the raw gorge. It flitted back and forth until it came up to the falling water from the lake; there it paused for a moment. It was the marten. The storm had driven him into the forest, and he had remained to take advantage of its casualties until the openness of the drop-off had attracted him. It had seemed like a good place to find wood rats, but he had been disappointed; the ground of the slope was too unstable for the brushy cover the rats liked.

He couldn't make up his mind which way to follow the stream, so he vacillated, moving a little way upstream, then down, and finally following the water over the lip of the hanging ravine. As soon as he came level with the skinny lake, he smelled fish. This wouldn't have interested him very much had he not had the opportunity, earlier in the summer, of sampling a trout that some fisherman on the upper lake had been saving for breakfast. It had been a strikingly convenient and satisfying meal, and he'd paid a lot more attention to lakes since then.

There was a campsite behind a bunch of willows, and he headed that way with excitement. But it was unoccupied—the circle of charred rocks was cold and smelled only faintly of fried fish. So he kept following the shore. A red-legged frog had been croaking (although it was cold enough to make the marten's breath cloudy), and as the marten passed its hiding place in the reeds, it plopped into the water. The marten paused again and peered into the lake.

Something moved near a half-submerged dead log. The marten peered out over the dark water, but the movement had subsided. The lake's surface was dotted with tiny cartoon faces consisting of two wide eyes and a round O of a mouth. The faces were the backswimmers, protruding their two hind legs and the tips of their abdomens above the surface for air. Moving along again, the marten smelled the Lincoln's sparrow eggs broken by the hail and located the nest in its hiding place among the flattened rushes. One of the eggs was still intact, but the birds had given up and were sleeping off the storm's terrors in the willow grove.

There was a movement over the center of the lake as if something was rising out of the water. It was a bat fluttering over the surface in pursuit of early insects. A little earlier the movement could not have been seen from the shore, but the first indirect rays of sunlight were reflecting almost invisibly from the sky. The marten didn't like being in the open during the day (there were golden eagles watching the mountains in summer), so he disappeared up the side of the ravine after finishing the eggs.

The stars disappeared quickly and quietly—something of an anticlimax considering how fiercely they'd shone a little earlier—though some stars on the southwestern horizon did seem to flare up defiantly before they went out. Robins began to sing as the sky above the eastern horizon turned red. At the meadow a mountain quail called, and the grouse (which had sneaked down from their tree when it was still dark) scratched and clucked like secretive chickens. When the red border had risen higher in the sky, the Steller's jays woke up.

At about the same moment that the red light changed the colors of the fir cones and bark from bluish green to purple and brown, the branches began to quiver with morning breezes. The sun-warmed, rising air tore at the small orb webs that had been constructed during the night and awoke a wandering impulse in some of the weavers. Instead of retreating into a cranny for the day, these spiders climbed to the tips of branches and spun a long thread of silk into the air until the breeze caught it and lifted them. Then they sailed away, climbing above the treetops into the sunlight which made the threads glitter and sparkle. It seemed as if strands of living light were drifting over the forest. The needle-miners that the spiders had spent the night trying to catch still fluttered about, showing dark against the sky now.

The buck that had fled at the bear's approach earlier appeared beside the lake at the same time the marten departed. He grazed peacefully in a small meadow at the upper end until the jays began to make a commotion in the forest above. Looking up, he couldn't see or smell anything to fear, but moved cautiously to the far edge of the meadow anyway. The jays had found the marten trying to dig out a chipmunk hole and were amusing themselves by screaming at him and diving over his head (always at a very safe distance). The chipmunk was screaming too, somewhat muffled in the depths of the hole, and a bleary-eyed Douglas squirrel jumped and scolded on a branch. Chickadees, juncos, nuthatches, warblers, and flycatchers watched in quiet fascination.

The marten gave up after a few minutes of this, but first he defecated fastidiously in the fresh earth he had excavated. If he couldn't have the chipmunk, he would at least leave his mark. Then he moved off, energetic as ever, checking each scent he crossed. The chipmunk shut up, and the jays looked disappointed and left, some of them following the marten to see what he would do next. But the Douglas squirrel kept scolding. He seemed to have worked himself into a state.

The Broken Surface

Shortly after the jays stopped screaming, the male of the spotted sandpiper pair nesting by the upper lake flew down the ravine and landed on the half-submerged log that earlier had caught the marten's attention. The sandpipers' nest had been somewhat protected by the cliff's overhang, so they hadn't lost their eggs in the storm. He stretched his wings, whistled a few times (the call sounded more cheerful in the first light than it had in the last), and then examined the log to see what the night had provided.

The sun rose above the top of the ravine, casting tree shadows diagonally across the western side of the ravine. Soil and branches touched by the slanting rays turned scarlet for a moment, and flies began to buzz as the warmth loosened their wing muscles. The light made it easy to distinguish the buck's coat from the ground, and he soon moved into the trees. The rain-soaked plants that the hail had flattened began to pop erect again.

The night was deceptively quiet until the lightning jumped the peaks; then it was cracked down the middle by a thick bolt of lightning.

The lowlands, visible through the gap at the end of the ravine, were still a deep blue, untouched by the sunlight. The shaggy marine color of the ponderosa pines contrasted sharply with the velvety, almost black chaparral, which contrasted in its turn with the powder blue of the foothills. The valley was a violet smear with a white streak of river fog down its middle, the streetlights turned off now. Beyond it, the Cascades glowed purple. Sunlit orange peaks floated in the dusty air.

The sandpiper on the log found two water striders, a ladybird beetle that had flown over from the willows, and a damselfly nymph that had just crawled out to undergo metamorphosis. As he fed, the fierce little sharp-shinned hawk from the ridge watched him. She had come to the lake for a drink. Sandpipers weren't her usual prey—she was best at running down finches and warblers in the forest—but the busy, speckle-breasted bird on the log seemed vulnerable. Leaving her perch, the hawk beat her wings a few times for speed and bulleted down toward him, ready for a chase into the trees where her short wings would outmaneuver his long ones.

The sandpiper saw her coming and cried out in alarm as he started to fly away over the water. But, like the sadness of his mate's evening whistle, the despair in his tone was deceptive; actually, he managed to evade the hawk neatly. Instead of flying into the trees, he flew down right into the water. Entering the placid lake with barely a splash, he folded his wings slightly and continued to "fly" underwater. The hawk had no way of countering this tactic—she could no more fly in water than walk on it. As far as she was concerned, the sandpiper had disappeared. She quickly lost interest and flew off. She didn't have time to waste on inexplicable behavior; it usually took several unsuccessful pursuits before she caught a meal.

The sandpiper "flew" across the little lake, driving the trout and backswimmers before him. Strings of silvery bubbles rose from his beak

102

and feathers, marking his progress as they drifted to the surface. It was hard work, and he burst back into the air before long, leaving a large ring spreading across the water. As the ring expanded and started to fade, it was punctured by smaller ones—the first trout strikes of the day. The sandpiper fluttered back up the ravine toward his nest; he was the one that did most of the egg sitting. Then the sunlight reached the lake surface, dissipating a thin mist and breaking its mirror smoothness into a million sparkling reflections.

In the shady depths there is the subdued
light of perpetual morning.
John Muir, *Our National Parks*

Honey Mushrooms and the Nature of Darkness

During the rainstorms of spring or fall, visitors to the lower altitudes of the Yolla Bollys may witness a phenomenon which, while not uncommon in wild places, has acquired a legendary aura because people so seldom walk through forests at night. It is foxfire, and the likelihood of seeing it depends somewhat on the quality of one's equipment. People with snug tents are likely to sleep through a downpour in relative comfort, while those with only a tube tent or tarp will probably spend the small hours of a nocturnal storm jumping up and down in the dark to keep warm.

This is when foxfire will be seen. At first it may be mistaken for the illusory pinpoints of light which deceive eyes unaccustomed to the dark;

then the watcher becomes aware of small chips of phosphorescence scattered over the oak leaf litter, like diminutive, greenish yellow embers. They may seem to wink on and off as the nerve cells of the eye attempt to adjust to this new experience but are quite real. They are luminous mycelium strands of the honey armillaria fungus growing on dead twigs and bits of bark and in the soil. By day they are mere blackish threads, virtually invisible; their light only becomes conspicuous to the human eye in the profound obscurity of a stormy night. The mushrooms of honey armillaria and of another fungus (appropriately called jack-o'-lanterns) are also phosphorescent and can sometimes be glimpsed from a distance in otherwise inky woodlands.

Foxfire has been suspect to humans perhaps because its glow, like some demon's lure or fairy's lamp, beckons not to more light but to greater darkness. But if foxfire doesn't exist to mock humanity or lead us astray, then why does it exist? To attract or repel nocturnal insects—to mock beetles or lead them astray? Nobody seems to know. It is one of those unexplained phenomena that inhabit the twilight of human consciousness. It is likely that there are more reasons for its existence than we can imagine, and it is certain that mushroom light is connected in numerous ways to the more highly regarded light of the stars, via our sun. In a sense, the same things might be said about darkness. It doesn't exist to lead us from the one true path; we don't, in fact, know why it exists; but we do know that it is connected to light.

Darkness occupies a peculiar place in the modern mind. Light is real, physical; it is studied, measured, and metered. The best of human thinking has gone into understanding light. Darkness, on the other hand, is assumed to be a primal condition, an absolute quality; to measure it would transgress every tenet of reason. It is simply that which came before—a curiously mystical concept for a scientific culture.

To common sense and popular science, of course, darkness is merely the absence of light, the emptiness between particles. Even so, it should be respected because we humans have such a limited perception of it. The darkness of night is not a void; it is half of life on earth. Most of what we call darkness is not really darkness at all, and the light we congratulate ourselves on bringing into it obscures the light that is already there. Foxfire would be the best lamp for explorations of the night; we would have to grow new eyes to see with it.

If I seem absent from the narrative, it's perhaps because I'm so omnipresent that the reader can't distinguish me from the background.

106

EPILOGUE

About Night Watching

Some of the events in this book are described just as I encountered them. Some have been rearranged or elaborated. Others have been invented from conversations with other observers, from natural history literature, or from conjecture, speculation, and other euphemisms for storytelling. I wanted to write a readable account of a wilderness night based largely on my own experience—five years of observations in various parts of northern California. Since this experience wasn't condensed or coherent enough to stimulate the reader's imagination, I've taken liberties. If I seem absent from the narrative, it's perhaps because I'm so omnipresent that the reader can't distinguish me from the background, as with those human figures that baroque painters used to contrive from vegetables, seafood, or mountain landscapes.

I didn't invent the Yolla Bollys of course. The foothills, canyons, ridges, forests, lakes, and peaks are more or less as I found them as I walked across the range. I drank a lot of warm, dusty water from pools in foothill creekbeds and was glad to get it. One of the more vivid pleasures of my life was reaching the first mountain spring after a night and morning in the chaparral with no water at all. Two loggers on a fishing trip gave me a ride for the last mile or so. I had just tied my pack to its frame with twine, the weight of food and field guides having parted them, and was literally hotfooting it from one small patch of shade to another—the dirt road became like a bed of coals soon after sunup. The loggers were both about seven feet tall, with arms and legs like tree limbs over which sunburnt red skin and blonde hairs had been stretched. I felt like a weedy species of vine sitting between them.

They were the first motorists I encountered after leaving the paved road from Red Bluff. I hadn't *planned* on walking to the Yolla Bollys through the foothills and chaparral. I had intended to confine my narrative to the wilderness area, but I became so interested in the foothill night that I widened my inquiries. Although I cursed every thirsty mile of it, the walk gave me a true appreciation of the relief night brings to the Upper Sonoran zone in July, and I'm glad I took it. It was as though the Yolla Bollys weren't satisfied that I should admire only their forests, meadows, and peaks. I must become acquainted with their nether regions as well—a kind of "inferno" before the "paradiso" of the high country. Of course the foothills and chaparral are not a hell, but a living world, a very beautiful one. "Love us, love our foothills," said the mountains.

So this would be a very different book if someone had given me a ride at the valley edge of the foothills. In fact, such accidents are probably the major force behind the book, since I'm mainly interested in writing about things I've seen, heard, touched, or otherwise experienced. This is by no means a definitive portrait of nocturnal ecology in the California mountains but a personal evocation. The reader who is disappointed at not encountering a ringtail or puma in these pages shares my own disappointment at never having run into these elusive creatures. I'm not sure disappointment is the right word. It would be a dull world if we knew everything in it. I might prefer the puma to remain always over the next ridge—a presence, a lurking possibility.

Accident was also responsible for my exploration of the logged area of the Transition zone. When the loggers dropped me at the spring, my feet were too blistered to carry the pack for several days. I spent the time blundering about the old logging roads at night, peering into culverts, puddles, seeps, thickets, gullies, and grassy spots, and generally making a nuisance of myself to the area's rightful inhabitants: moths, spiders, beetles, toads, bats, and such. A spelunker's headlamp which I'd brought could light up an animal's eyes at an impressive distance, as though a small pair of headlights had suddenly been turned on in some inky grove. It was less useful at close quarters though, and I felt a little ridiculous shooting such a powerful beam of light into the inoffensive darkness. So I generally fell back on my usual method of night exploration—sitting, standing, or walking about in the dark. (If I lay down, I fell asleep.) A small flashlight could be used to elucidate details such as spider webs or rattlesnakes. I didn't have a red light, not being the inventive sort, but most of the creatures paid little attention to me anyway.

I met the small, peculiar-looking bear described in "The Sugar Pine" section beside a logging road at daybreak. He was in a patch of oak scrub across a gully, and I was upwind. I don't think he could see me. He somehow became uneasy, though, and his nose began to twitch. A distinct expression of alarm overspread his features. Then there was a crashing noise in the brush, and he was gone—zip!—as if some cosmic force had sucked him away.

The large bear of "The Foxtail Pine" section, which I encountered in the wilderness area, was indeed very large, or seemed so in the moonless dark. He was peaceable, however, and gave me only a cursory glance as he moved along his bear trail. His eyes gleamed quite an impressive red, then turned suddenly to green, as though they were stoplights. The gopher-hunting coyote wasn't observed in the Yolla Bollys at all but in Lassen National Park. His encounter with the bear was suggested by an aggressive bear I saw chasing two smaller bears in the Yosemite backcountry, and by accounts of bears bullying coyotes. Likewise, the episode of the two does treeing the small bear was suggested by numerous accounts of deer chasing and treeing bobcats, and by occasions when I've stumbled on a doe with a new fawn. The doe hesitates, obviously torn between fear of man and a strong aggressive urge.

Lassen Park was also where I saw a pine marten mobbed by jays while trying to dig a chipmunk out of its burrow. In the Trinity Alps, about seventy miles north of the Yolla Bollys, martens came into my camps on two occasions. One actually rummaged through my cooking pots as I lay in my sleeping bag, and the other clearly considered doing so but thought better of it because I happened to be using them at the time. So although I didn't happen to meet a pine marten in the Yolla Bollys, I had to put one there. It is within suitable range and habitat, and the high country didn't seem complete without one.

Much more frustrating to write about than such uncommon but spectacular animals as bears and martens are animals which are quite common in suitable habitat but very difficult to see. Dusky-footed wood rats and northern flying squirrels are good examples. I often stood for hours in the dark surrounded by a furtive cacophony of rattles, rustles, squeakings, and scoldings but saw no more than the faintest hints of movement, even when I beamed the flashlight on very close noises. It was like being surrounded by elves. Sometimes I was startled by whirring sounds directly overhead. These sounds were distinct but so soft that they seemed unreal—dreamlike—a few moments after they had occurred. I finally confirmed my suspicion that flying squirrels were doing this when an individual landed on a nearby tree trunk after gliding over my head and scolded me for several moments. Its eyes reflected a pinkish light, like rose quartz.

Sometimes I moved animals from one part of the Yolla Bollys to another, although I never moved them out of suitable habitat unless, as with the porcupine in the chaparral and the jackrabbit in the forest, I found them there. The hermit thrush which I describe singing near the lake was actually heard in an exceptionally fine grove of white fir just outside the wilderness area. After listening for an hour to this Caruso of hermit thrushes, I walked on a few steps and ran into a line of red plastic ribbons for a newly surveyed logging road. The thrush's grove was about to be cut out from under him. I've moved him into the wilderness so he can keep singing, at least on paper.

I was less cavalier in my treatment of plants, invertebrates, and other easily watched beings. The Yolla Bollys provide a dependable supply of insects, spiders, and myriapods, not to mention frogs, toads, and newts, so there is not as much legerdemain with such creatures as with the larger animals. The same is true of scenery, sunsets, moonscapes, dawns, and other atmospheric effects, although there are some bits of other northern California wildlands scattered about.

The storm was a real Yolla Bolly hailstorm. Of course I didn't observe it from all three life zones at once. As I cowered in a dry meadow gully, its thunder and lightning literally shook the ground and blew a nearby large ponderosa pine to pieces. The lightning also started a fire on the next ridge, hastening my departure from that particular campsite. When I eventually ran out of food and started hitchhiking home (with another moonlight stroll through the chaparral), a member of the local forest fire unit gave me a ride in his air-conditioned, tape-decked Datsun. I mentioned the fire, and he complained rather bitterly about their difficulties fighting fires in the roadless Yolla Bolly-Middle Eel Wilderness. They had to walk or parachute in, if the fires couldn't be put out from the air. Since he was driving, I didn't tell him I preferred fires to fire roads in the Yolla Bollys, merely said something ingenuous about fires being what happened in wilderness. This inconclusive exchange has stuck in my mind. It seemed that we were both missing the point somehow in disagreeing about forest fires—as though humans had much definitive control over them, in or out of wilderness areas. We were like the blind men disagreeing about the elephant. Of course, I have no idea what the missed

111

point might be, and I still think the Yolla Bollys need fires—to keep their glades and groves open—and need protection from roads to keep their pumas and two-hundred-foot sugar pines alive.

I brought no special qualifications to my nocturnal forays. I don't have catlike eyes, and I've discovered no psychic powers except perhaps a healthy timidity which makes me very cautious when I feel uneasy. I hold no biology degrees. The knowledge I've used is accessible to anybody who's willing to poke around in libraries and biological abstracts, with a little pestering of biologists on the side. And I should confess that I never was able to stay up for a night without drifting off to sleep for at least a few minutes during the small hours. It's really very difficult to stay awake without bright light or some other form of stimulation. It was particularly hard in the cold, eerie high country night. A couple of times I crawled into my sleeping bag with the rationalization that it was "just to get warm for a minute" and woke up at the glow of dawn.

Some naturalists object to fictional treatment of animals and plants, which they call "nature faking." There is much to be said for this viewpoint. Facts are hard to come by. The fact finders may understandably resent the enthusiast who drags their carefully collected data into the hinterland of imagination.

But facts are only part of a humane relationship with the biosphere; feelings are just as important because they dictate behavior. The fact that the thread of humanity is woven into the living fabric of animals, plants, soils, waters, and winds won't be acted upon until most humans can feel this relationship. The old cultures translated an awareness of interdependence into myths that extended human feelings throughout the fabric, but the insulated existence of civilization numbs this awareness and the myths lose their meaning. We need new ways of connecting human sympathies to our nonhuman relatives. Fiction, the myth-making of an industrial age, is one way.

112

Civilization no longer needs to open up wilderness; it needs wilderness to help open up the still largely unexplored human mind. Two things are required to fill this need: We must have access to wilderness and, equally important, wilderness must have access to us. The first requirement is met with trail guides and backpacks; the second is more problematic. It is not so easy to pay attention to wild places when they are distant from our daily lives and can only be visited for a few weeks of the year. So guides for the imagination are also useful, not to speak *for* wilderness—it says different things to different people—but to suggest some ways of listening to it.

Bibliography

ANTHONY, H. E. *Field Book of North American Mammals.* G. P. Putnam's Sons, New York, 1928.

BAKKER, Elna. *An Island Called California.* University of California Press, Berkeley, 1971.

BATES, Marston. *The Natural History of Mosquitoes.* Harper and Row, New York, 1965.

BENT, Arthur C. *Life Histories of North American Shorebirds: Part II.* Dover, New York, 1962.

BORROR, Donald J., and White, Richard E. *A Field Guide to the Insects of America North of Mexico.* Houghton Mifflin Co., Boston, 1970.

BROWN, Vinson. *Knowing the Outdoors in the Dark.* Stackpole Books, Harrisburg, Pa., 1972.

BRYANT, Harold C. Nocturnal Wanderings of the California Pocket Gopher. *University of California Publications in Zoology,* vol. 12, no. 2, pp. 25-29, Nov. 20, 1913.

BURT, William Henry, and Grossenheider, Richard. *A Field Guide to the Mammals.* Houghton Mifflin Co., Boston, 1959.

CARR, Donald E. *The Forgotten Senses.* Doubleday and Co., Garden City, New York, 1972.

CARRIGHAR, Sally. *One Day on Beetle Rock.* Alfred A. Knopf, New York, 1945.

DIXON, Joseph. Notes on the Natural History of the Bushy Tailed Wood Rats of California. *University of California Publications in Zoology,* vol. 21, no. 3, pp. 49-74, Dec. 10, 1919.

ESSIG, E. O. *Insects of Western North America.* Macmillan and Co., New York, 1926.

FABRE, Henri. *The Life of the Spider.* Dodd, Mead and Co., New York, 1914.

———. *The Glow Worm and Other Beetles.* Dodd, Mead and Co., New York, 1919.

GRINNELL, Hilda Wood. A Synopsis of the Bats of California. *University of California Publications in Zoology,* January, 1918.

GRINNELL, Joseph; Dixon, J. S.; and Linsdale, J. M. *Fur Bearing Mammals of California.* University of California Press, Berkeley, 1937.

GOULD, Gordon I. The Status of the Spotted Owl in California (unpublished manuscript). California Department of Fish and Game and U.S. Forest Service, 1974.

HINDS, Norman E. A. *Evolution of the California Landscape.* State of California Department of Natural Resources Bulletin No. 158, San Francisco, 1952.

HUTCHINS, Ross E. *Insects*. Prentice-Hall, Englewood Cliffs, New Jersey, 1966.

JOHNSTON, Verna R. *The Sierra Nevada*. Houghton Mifflin Co., Boston, 1970.

LEE, Anthony Kingston. The Adaptions to Arid Environments in Wood Rats of the Genus *Neotoma. University of California Publications in Zoology*, vol. 64, no. 2, pp. 57-96, 1963.

LEVI, Herbert W. and Lorna R. *A Guide to Spiders and Their Kin*. Golden Press, New York, 1968.

LINSDALE, Jean M., and Tevis, Lloyd P., Jr. *The Dusky Footed Wood Rat*. University of California Press, Berkeley, 1951.

LOOMIS, Frederick B. *Physiography of the United States*. Doubleday, Doran and Co., New York, 1938.

MILNE, Lorus J. and Margery J. *The World of Night*. Viking Press, New York, 1956.

MUUL, Illar. Behavioral and Physiological Influences on the Distribution of the Flying Squirrel *Glaucomys Volans. Miscellaneous Publications of the Museum of Zoology*, no. 134, Feb. 2, 1962. University of Michigan, Ann Arbor.

NEEDHAM, James G., and Lloyd, J. T. *The Life of Inland Waters*. Charles C.Thomas Co., Springfield, Illinois, 1930.

Ross, Anthony. Ecological Aspects of the Food Habits of Insectivorous Bats. *Proceedings of the Western Foundation of Vertebrate Zoology*, vol. 1, no. 4, May,1967.

Ross, Edward S. *Insects Close-up*. University of California Press, Berkeley, 1953.

STORER, Tracy I., and Usinger, Robert L. *Sierra Nevada Natural History: An Illustrated Handbook*. University of California Press, Berkeley, 1971.

TRASK, Dr. John D. *Report on the Geology of the Coast Mountains*. Document No. 9, California Senate, 1854.

WALLS, Gordon Lynn. *The Vertebrate Eye and Its Adaptive Radiation*. Cranbrook Institute of Science, Bulletin No. 19, 1942.

WARD, Ritchie R. *The Living Clocks*. Alfred A. Knopf, New York, 1971.

116

Index to Animals and Plants

ily Carabidæ. They are caterpillar hunters and predators on many insect pests. 26, 29, 52, 96

BEETLE, LONG-HORNED, family Cerambycidæ. A large family characterized by antennæ at least half as long as the body, often much longer. Larvæ bore in dead or dying plants. 30, 53

BEETLE, PREDACIOUS DIVING, family Dytiscidæ. Streamlined. Row through the water by moving hind feet in unison. 12, 59

BEETLE, WATER SCAVENGER, family Hydrophilidæ. Similar to predacious diving beetles but swim by moving hind feet alternately. 50, 59, 97

BEETLE, WESTERN PINE, *Dendroctonus brevicomis*, family Scolytidæ. Adults and larvæ feed on ponderosa bark, excavating many-branched channels. 56

BLEEDING HEART, *Dicentra formosa*, Fumitory Family. Rose purple blossoms resemble tiny bleeding hearts. 47

BLUEBIRD, WESTERN, *Sialia mexicana*, Thrush Family. Resembles eastern bluebird—blue back, red breast. 49

BLUEBLOSSOM, *Ceanothus thyrsiflorus*, Buckthorn Family. A blue-flowered member of a large genus of evergreen shrubs with many-ribbed leaves and fragrant clusters of tiny blossoms. 68

BOAR, RUSSIAN, *Sus scrofa*. Wild boar. Tusked, shaggy wild pig ranging from China to Europe. In California, introduced near Monterey and has spread to hills east of San Jose. Feral pigs, also found in coast ranges, are from escaped or liberated domestic breeds. 6

BUCKEYE, CALIFORNIA, *Aesculus californica*, Horse-chestnut Family. Shiny brown nuts are poisonous, but California Indians ate them after leaching out the alkaloids. 14, 22

BUDWORM. Larva of moths of the family Tortricidæ. 95

BUMBLEBEE, subfamily Apinæ, tribe Bombini. Native to North America, unlike honeybees. Mostly nest in ground. 48, 83

BUTTERCUP, genus *Ranunculus*, Buttercup Family. Crowfoot. Large group of perennial herbs. Flowers with five to seven glossy yellow or white petals. Leaves palmate and deeply cut. 76

CEDAR, INCENSE, *Libocedrus decurrens*, Cypress Family. Aromatic wood, frond-like foliage and fibrous, cinnamon-colored bark. 45, 57, 63, 65, 71, 76, 96

CENTIPEDE, genus *Scolopendra*, class Chilopoda. More or fewer than one hundred legs. All three thousand known species have poison glands opening through jaws. 54

CHAMISE, *Adenostoma fasciculatum*, Rose Family. Greasewood. Commonest chaparral shrub. Both gray green leaves and white flowers are tiny. 14

CHICKADEE, *Parus gambeli*. Mountain chickadee. The resident species of mountain forests in the far West. A white stripe over the eye. 70, 100

CHIPMUNK, genus *Eutamias*. Some nine

species in California alone. 50, 100, 110

CICADA, family Cicadidæ. Related to aphids and leafhoppers, cicadas spend winters underground as brown nymphs, sucking plant roots. The buzzing of males is a part of summer almost everywhere. 12, 81

CINQUEFOIL, genus *Potentilla*, Rose Family. White or yellow, five-petaled flowers and five- or three-parted leaves. Resemble wild strawberries but don't produce berries. 76

COFFEEBERRY, *Rhamnus californica*, Buckthorn Family. Black berries are extremely bitter. 17

COLUMBINE, *Aquilegia truncata*, Buttercup Family. Red columbine. Blossoms resemble clusters of tiny, hovering doves. Moist, shaded spots. 64

COTTONWOOD, genus *Populus*, Willow Family. Fast-growing, short-lived trees named for the cottony hairs on the seeds. 12, 36

COYOTE, *Canis latrans*. As in other parts of North America, coyotes have apparently taken advantage of widespread logging and moved into California's north coast forests in greater numbers than formerly (as if to compensate for government control programs which killed over 500,000 in California from 1891 to 1972, at an estimated $30 million cost to taxpayers). 36, 38, 69, 87, 109

CREEPER, *Certhia familiaris*. Brown creeper. Small, curved-billed bird common but inconspicuous in North American forests. Creeps spirally up trees seeking insects. 49

CRICKET, CAMEL, genus *Ceuthophilus*, subfamily Raphidophorinæ. In dark places throughout North America. 89

CRICKET, FIELD, genus *Gryllus*, subfamily Gryllinæ. The familiar house cricket. 16, 30

CRICKET, GROUND, genus *Nemobius*, subfamily Nemobiinæ. 38, 52, 54

CRICKET, JERUSALEM, genus *Stenopelmatus*, subfamily Stenopelmatinæ. Mainly along Pacific seaboard. Relation to Jerusalem unclear. 37, 54

CRICKET, TREE, genus *Oecanthus*, subfamily Oecanthinæ. Many species. Some chirp, most trill. 17, 31, 38, 52

CURRANT, GOLDEN, *Ribes aureum*, Saxifrage Family. Edible berries. 68

DADDY LONGLEGS, genus *Phalangium*, family Phalangiidæ. Harvestmen. Not spiders, although related. Lack poison and silk. Eat plant matter or small insects. 23, 30, 56

DAMSELFLY, suborder Zygoptera. Resemble dragonflies but are more slender and hold wings together above body, instead of horizontal, when at rest. 54, 102

DEER, BLACK-TAILED, *Odocoileus hemionus*. Mule deer. Black-tailed deer of Pacific Coast, was once regarded as a separate species but is now seen as a subspecies of the mule deer common throughout the West. 16, 53, 60, 68, 86, 99, 110

DESMIDS, order Zygnematales. Unicellular or colonial green algæ. 79

DIATOMS, order Diatomaceæ. Siliceous, single-celled algæ. Beautiful, glasslike patterns and colors. 79

DRAGONFLY, suborder Anisoptera. Wings held horizontal at rest. Green darner, *Anax junius*, is a common, large species. 12, 14, 22

EAGLE, GOLDEN, *Aquila chrysætos*. The bird of Jove lives mainly on rabbits and ground squirrels; weighs eight to thirteen pounds. 99

ERIOGONUM, SULFUR-FLOWERED, *Eriogonum umbellatum*, Buckwheat Family. Named for the sulfur yellow color of the blossom, not the smell. 76

EUGLENOIDS, genus *Euglena*. Single-celled algæ that move about with whiplike flagella. 79

FINCH, PURPLE, *Carpodacus purpureus*. Peterson's *A Field Guide to the Western Birds* likens this species to "a sparrow dipped in raspberry juice." 49, 102

FIR, RED, *Abies magnifica*, Pine Family. California red fir. True firs are distinguished from spruce, hemlock, and Douglas fir by large, upright cones. Red fir cones are a deep violet color when mature. Sierras and northern California. 76, 82, 88

FIR, WHITE, *Abies concolor*, Pine Family. Much more widely distributed than red fir—Sierras, south Cascades, south and central Rockies. 45, 57, 58, 65, 76, 77, 111

FLEA, order Siphonaptera. Wingless, laterally flattened insects with blood-sucking mouthparts. They are parasites of birds and mammals. About eleven hundred known species. 25, 34

FLY, BLACK, family Simuliidæ, order Diptera. Bites of these tiny flies can be dangerously debilitating in muskeg, where they are abundant. They're fortunately less numerous elsewhere. 77

FLY, CRANE, family Tipulidæ, order Diptera. Mature individuals feed on other insects, plants, or not at all, depending on the species. Maggotlike larvæ live in moist ground or streams, eat plant material. 50

FLY, DEER, family Tabanidæ, order Diptera. As with mosquitoes, females bite (painfully) and suck blood to provide nourishment for egg-laying. Males eat nectar and pollen. Family includes horseflies. 12, 83

FLYCATCHER, OLIVE-SIDED, *Nuttallornis borealis*. A large, bullheaded flycatcher. Whistled song has been transcribed as "hic, three beers!" 95, 100

FORGET-ME-NOT, genus *Myosotis*, Borage Family. There are many species of this blue-petalled, yellow-centered wildflower. 76

FOX, GRAY, *Urocyon cinereoargenteus*. Common fox of brush and forest from the northern United States to Tierra del Fuego. Readily climbs trees. 34

FROG, PACIFIC TREE, *Hyla regilla*. Only tree frog native to northern California.

May be brown, green, reddish, tan, gray, or black depending on surroundings. Black stripe along side of head. 25, 56, 63

FROG, REDLEGGED, *Rana aurora*. Classified in same genus as bullfrog and leopard frog, this West Coast species has red skin on the insides of its hind legs. Breeds in June and July. 98

FUNGUS, HONEY ARMILLARIA. *Armillaria mellea*, honey mushroom, oak fungus. Mushrooms are one to six inches across, pale to dark brown. Stem honey colored. Root parasite on oak and peach trees. Edible. 104

FUNGUS, JACK-O-LANTERN, *Clitocybe illudens*. Deceiving clitocybe. On hardwood logs and stumps. Not fatal if eaten but very nauseating. 104

FUNGUS, PUFFBALL, class Gasteromycetes. Large group characterized by a membrane (peridium) over spore-bearing surface. Rounded, pale-colored puffballs easily recognized. Most (but not all) are edible. Also includes stinkhorns, earth stars. 92

FUNGUS, RAINBOW SHELF, *Polyporus versicolor*. Spore-bearing pores are located under shelflike, multicolored fruiting bodies. 30

FUNGUS, TRUFFLE, class Ascomycetes. Several dozen species of underground fruiting fungi. Same group as prized edible morels. 92

FUNGUS, WHITE POUCH, *Cryptoporus volvatus*. Grows on conifers except junipers and sequoia. 56

GNAT, family Chironomidæ, order Diptera. Midge. Tiny, mosquitolike flies. Swarms of males attract females for mating. 16, 22, 49, 77

GOOSEBERRY, genus *Ribes*, Saxifrage Family. Like closely related currants, the several gooseberry species have palmate leaves and edible berries. Some have prickly berries, which seems an odd way of encouraging animals to eat them and spread the seeds. 54

GOPHER, POCKET, genus *Thomomys*. Named for fur-lined, external cheek pouches used to carry loose earth or food. Large front incisors and curved claws make gophers efficient burrowers. Their constant turning of soil has probably contributed greatly to soil fertility in the earthworm-poor West. Farmers detest them anyway. 87

GRAPE, WILD, *Vitis californica*, Vine Family. This species has toothed, heart-shaped leaves and purple berries. Climbs mainly on oak and cottonwood in foothills and valley. Tiny flowers are very fragrant. 12, 25

GRASSHOPPER, BAND-WINGED, subfamily Oedipodinæ, family Acrididæ. This family, the short-horned (short-antennaed) grasshoppers, includes most of the common, daytime grasshoppers. Band-winged is named for the brightly colored hind wings which flash when the individual flies. 40, 78

GRASSHOPPER, SHIELD-BACKED, subfamily Decticinæ, family Tettigoniidæ. This family, the long-horned grasshoppers, includes the katydids common in eastern woodlands. The famous "Mormon cricket" is actually a shield-backed grasshopper. 19, 33

GROUND SQUIRREL, CALIFORNIA, *Spermophilus beecheyi*. Digger squirrel. This common species of foothill and valley has been vastly persecuted because of crop damage and because the fleas in some of its burrows have become infected with bubonic plague since white takeover of California. Plague has been spread from its original niche in the marmot burrows of Mongolia to rodent burrows in many parts of the world. 13

GROUND SQUIRREL, GOLDEN-MANTLED, *Spermophilus lateralis*. Striped like a chipmunk but distinguishable by its larger size, coppery head and shoulders, and lack of stripes on face. 49

GROUSE, DUSKY, *Dendragapus obscurus*. Blue grouse. Dusky gray or blackish grouse of western conifer forest. 82, 99

HAWK, COOPER's, *Accipiter cooperi*. A short-winged, long-tailed raptor. Generally darts after prey through trees and thickets. Adults have blue gray backs and rusty breasts. Crow size. 50

HAWK, RED-TAILED, *Buteo jamaicensis*. Common soaring hawk of North America, with broad wings and a rounded tail which is rufous on top. Watches for small mammals from high in air, then descends to a perch from which to launch its attack. 13, 15, 40

HAWK, SHARP-SHINNED, *Accipiter striatus*. Like a small Cooper's hawk, except for square-ended, notched tail. Jay size. Male Cooper's may be same size as the female sharp-shinned hawk. Both species threatened in varying degrees. 77, 102

HOSACKIA, *Lotus torreyi*, Pea Family. Meadow hosackia. 47, 49, 53

JACKRABBIT, BLACK-TAILED, *Lepus californicus*. Actually a hare. Young are born fully furred with eyes open; they soon hop after mother. 38, 65, 111

JAY, SCRUB, *Aphelocoma cœrulescens*, California jay. Uncrested jay of foothills and brush throughout West. Blue head, wings, and tail. Brown back. 16, 24, 40

JAY, STELLER's, *Cyanocitta stelleri*. Crested jay of western forests. Head and shoulders black, the rest indigo blue. 47, 49, 99

JUNCO, *Junco oreganus*, Oregon junco. Common black-headed, brown-bodied member of the Sparrow Family. Nests in forests, winters in valleys. 49, 70, 100

KINGBIRD, WESTERN, *Tyrannus verticalis*. Along with phoebes, pewees, and flycatchers, a member of the Tyrant Flycatcher Family. 14

LANIATORE, suborder Laniatores, order Opiliones. A mainly tropical group of harvestmen. A few species in the western and southern United States. 24

LARKSPUR, TALL, *Delphinium glaucum*, Buttercup Family. Three to six feet tall in moist places. 59

LARVA, CADDIS FLY, order Trichoptera. Caddis worm. Adult caddis flies are mothlike insects with long, jointed antennæ. Aquatic larvæ are grublike, protect themselves in silken cases covered with pebbles, pine needles, twigs, or other material, according to species. 52

LARVA, GNAT, family Chironomidæ. Bloodworms. Red color is caused by hemoglobin. An important trout food. 52

LAUREL, *Umbellularia californica*, Laurel Family. California laurel, bay laurel, Oregon myrtle, pepperwood. Aromatic evergreen leaves, purple fruit, small but fragrant greenish white flowers. 12, 16, 36, 40

LEAFHOPPER, family Cicadellidæ. Colorful relatives of cicadas and aphids. 16, 79

LICHEN, WOLF, *Letharia vulpina*. Staghorn lichen. Abundant fruticose lichen on conifers. Thin, many-branching, yellow green thallus. As with all lichens, made up of a species of alga and a species of fungus. 49

LILY, CORN, *Veratrum californicum*, Lily Family. False hellebore. Stout, leafy stems resemble cornstalks. 47, 50, 58, 76, 86

LILY, LEOPARD, *Lilium pardalinum*, Lily Family. Resembles tiger lily but is larger. 47

LIZARD, ALLIGATOR, genus *Gerrhonotus*. Big-headed lizards reaching a body length of six inches, the tail twice as long. Upper surface gray or olive with dark markings. Rather sedate unless unduly pestered, then they run away wriggling on small legs. Will bite, harmlessly, but main defense (as with many reptiles) is to empty bowels on tormentor. 25, 34

LIZARD, FENCE, *Sceloporus occidentalis*. Swift, bluebelly. A very common brown or gray lizard found in most relatively dry habitats. Body and tail together measure five to nine inches. Males have conspicuous blue patches on sides and throat (females sometimes with lesser blue patches). During mating season, much doing of "push ups," an aggressive display of blue patches, and general chasing back and forth. 48

LOOPER, family Geometridæ. Geometer, measuring worm. A moth caterpillar that moves by humping its body into a loop. 30, 95

LUPINE, genus *Lupinus*, Pea Family. Purple, blue, yellow, white, and pink flowered species. Thrives on poor soil because of nitrogen-fixing bacteria associated with roots. Name from Latin *lupus*—wolf—derives from Roman misconception that plants ravaged soil fertility, when it was really the Romans themselves. 75, 76, 83, 87

MANZANITA, genus *Arctostaphylos*, Heath Family. Bearberry. Evergreen shrubs with ovoid leaves and white or pink, urn-shaped blossoms. Name from Spanish *manzana*—apple—because berries look (but don't taste) like tiny apples. Dozens of species in California. 14, 22, 46, 48, 52

MAPLE, BIG-LEAF, *Acer macrophyllum*, Maple Family. Broad-leaf maple. The only large maple on the West Coast. 45

MARTEN, PINE, *Martes americana*. Marten. Formerly throughout Rockies, Cascades, Sierra Nevada, and Northwest Coast but much reduced by trapping in past, by predator poisoning and habitat destruction today. Eurasian sable is related. 81, 91, 97, 110

MAYFLY, order Ephemeroptera. Delicate insects that live in their adult, winged form only long enough to mate. Nymphs are aquatic. Adults and nymphs have two or three long "tails" at end of abdomen. Were often astonishingly abundant in rivers and lakes before widespread pollution. 77, 78, 80

MILLIPEDE, genus *Spirobolus*, class Diplopoda. This genus has in the vicinity of two hundred legs. 89

MISTLETOE, CEDAR, *Phoradendron juniperinum libocedri*, Mistletoe Family. The orange color of this dicot shows its parasitic nature. Lives on incense cedar. 49, 62

MITE, order Acarina. A large group of tiny arachnids (spider relatives). Many species parasitic on plants or animals. Includes chiggers, spider mites, ear mites. 25, 86

MITE, RED WATER, *Limnochares americana*. An aquatic, predacious mite. 79

MONKEY-FLOWER, SCARLET, *Mimulus cardinalis*, Snapdragon Family. Tubed flow-

ers end in five lobes with alleged resemblance to a monkey face. Wet places. 54, 64

MONKEY-FLOWER, STICKY, genus *Diplacus*, Snapdragon Family. Bush monkey-flower. Yellow or orange flowered shrubs of chaparral. 14

MOSQUITO, TREEHOLE, genus *Aedes*. Adults lay eggs in decayed holes in trees in summer. Winter rains fill holes with water and larvæ hatch. 12

MOTH, NEEDLE-MINER, family Gelechiidæ. Miniscule larvæ tunnel into conifer needles, killing them. Entire forests of lodgepole pine may be killed by infestations. Lodgepoles tend to grow in unmixed stands—the perils of uniformity. 53, 81, 99

MOTH, NOCTUID, family Noctuidæ. Owlet moth. The commonest moths. Most adults feed on flower nectar. Larvæ include cutworms, armyworms, earworms. 56, 69

MOTH, PINE LOOPER, *Phengommatœa edwardsata*, family Geometridæ. 52

MOTH, PLUME, family Pterophoridæ. Wings are cleft and plumelike. 59

MOUSE, BRUSH, *Peromyscus boylii*. Big-eyed, big-eared, white-footed mouse of foothills. 25, 29

MOUSE, DEER, *Peromyscus maniculatus*. May be commonest wild mammal in North America. Mexico to Alaska. All mice of genus *Peromyscus* look similar. Very pretty little rodents but bite earnestly if cornered. Also can abscond with a week's supply of sunflower seeds and raisins in one night, with much scampering over the sleeping owner's face in the process. 58, 60, 62, 92

Mouse, meadow, genus *Microtus*. Field mouse, meadow vole. Large group of small-eyed, small-eared, mainly short-tailed rodents of grassy places. Boom and bust population cycles. 2, 53, 68

Nettle. A coarse, herbaceous plant, usually of the Nettle Family (Urticaceæ) but term is also used for some Mint Family plants. The alien stinging nettle, common in waste places or on river-banks, provides an unforgettable intro-duction to the Nettle Family. 54, 86

Newt, rough-skinned, *Taricha granulosa*. One of several species of this semi-aquatic genus of salamanders in California. Spend cold weather underground, then travel to water to spawn. 59, 111

Nightshade, *Solanum xantii*, Potato Family. Purple nightshade. Has blue flowers, light green berries. Poisonous to humans. 33

Nuthatch, *Sitta carolinensis*. White-breasted nuthatch. Only birds that hab-itually walk down a tree trunk head first. Most of North America. 12, 100

Nymph, damselfly, suborder Zygop-tera. Aquatic immature form. Has three leaflike gills at end of abdomen. 102

Oak, blue, *Quercus douglasii*, Beech Family. Deciduous. Leaves oval, either smooth-margined or five-lobed. 11, 46

Oak, California black, *Quercus kel-*

loggii, Beech Family. Deciduous. Toothed, five- to seven-lobed leaves. 45, 65

Oak, golden-cup, *Quercus chrysolepsis*, Beech Family. Canyon live oak. Ever-green. Smooth-margined or toothed leaves have yellowish undersides. Acorns have hairy yellow cups. 45

Oak, live, *Quercus wislizenii*, Beech Family. Interior live oak. Evergreen. Leaves smooth-margined or toothed. 11, 15, 24, 28

Oak, valley, *Quercus lobata*, Beech Family. California white oak. Decidu-ous. Smooth-margined, seven- to eleven-lobed leaves. Elongated acorns. Largest western oak. Threatened by overgraz-ing, suburbanization, and other pres-sures. To 120 feet tall. 11

Onion, wild, genus *Allium*, Lily Fam-ily. Several species, with round pink or white flower heads. 53

Orchid, rein, *Habenaria dilatata*, Or-chid Family. Boreal bog orchid. 59

Owl, burrowing, *Speotyto cunicularia*. Grasslands throughout West. Ground squirrel and prairie dog eradication threatens this species. 40, 70

Owl, great horned, *Bubo virginianus*. Common large owl throughout North America (except tundra). 16, 21, 36, 40, 58, 63

Owl, pygmy, *Glaucidium gnoma*. A small owl without ear tufts. Wooded moun-tains of West. 70

Owl, screech, *Otus asio*. A small owl with ear tufts, common throughout

United States. Oaks and river bottom of foothills in California. 33

OWL, SPOTTED, *Strix occidentalis*. A rare species of western mature forest, or rather a species of the increasingly rare mature forest. 55, 57, 60, 62

PAINTBRUSH, INDIAN, genus *Castilleja*, Snapdragon Family. Scarlet "blossoms" are bracts and calyx. Petals and other flower parts are tiny and greenish. Some species parasitic. 64

PENNYROYAL, WESTERN, *Monardella odoratissima*, Mint Family. A wildflower specifically adapted to attract moths. 52, 76

PENSTEMON, genus *Penstemon*, Snapdragon Family. A large genus of colorful wildflowers. 76

PEWEE, WOOD, *Contopus sordidulus*. Western wood pewee. A medium-sized flycatcher of woods and forests from Alaska to Texas. Winters in South America. 71

PHOEBE, *Sayornis nigricans*, black phoebe. A black, white-bellied flycatcher resident in the Southwest, near water—canyons, streams, farmyards. 12

PIGEON, BAND-TAILED, *Columba fasciata*. A blue-bodied, purple-headed western wild pigeon with a light band at end of tail. Same size and shape as city pigeon, but rarely seen away from wild, isolated canyons, where swirling flocks above the oak woodland give an Edenic impression. 36

PIKA, *Ochotona princeps*, cony. A short-eared, alpine relative of the rabbit. Lives in rockslides and squeaks a lot. Puts out little piles of grass and flowers to cure in the sun for hay. 82

PINE, DIGGER, *Pinus sabiniana*, Pine Family. Stiff, gray green needles in bundles of three, eight to ten inches long. Indians ate seeds from large cones. 6, 14, 36, 47

PINE, FOXTAIL, *Pinus balfouriana*. Bundles of five needles, one to two inches long, remain on branches ten to twelve years, giving bushy "foxtail" appearance. Confined to Klamath highland, southern Sierra Nevada. 7, 83

PINE, LODGEPOLE, *Pinus contorta*. Bundles of two needles, one to three inches long. Cones remain closed on branches for years, open when heated. A fire-ecology species, widely distributed. 75, 83

PINE, PONDEROSA, *Pinus ponderosa*. Yellow pine. Bundles of two or three needles, five to ten inches long, form tufts near ends of branches. To 180 feet tall. 45, 54, 57, 75, 76, 82, 96, 102, 111

PINE, SUGAR, *Pinus lambertiana*. Twisted bundles of five needles, three to five inches long. Cones to twenty-six inches long. Tallest American pine—175 to 200 feet. Sugary sap. 7, 57, 69

POISON OAK, *Rhus diversiloba*, Sumac Family. Erect, spreading or climbing shrub. Three-parted leaves are rounded, lobed, or toothed. Oily substance in leaves, twigs, and other parts causes dermatitis in humans, as with poison ivy of East (*Rhus radicans*). Berries an important wildlife food. Grows up to five thousand feet elevation. 12, 25, 26, 33

PONDWEED, genus *Potamogeton*, Pondweed Family. Water plants with broad, oval floating leaves and slender, grasslike submerged leaves. 59

POOR-WILL, *Phalœnoptilus nuttallii*. A robin-sized, big-headed black, gray, and brown bird. Wide, bristle-fringed mouth an efficient trap for flying insects. Nests on ground. 24, 36, 54, 96

PORCUPINE, *Erethizon dorsatum*. This large, spiny rodent has been extirpated from many parts of the United States. 46, 64, 65, 111

PROTOZOANS, phylum Protozoa. Acellular or unicellular (but far from simple or primitive) animals. 79

PUMA, *Felis concolor*, mountain lion, cougar. The best friend a deer population ever had. 108

QUAIL, CALIFORNIA, *Lophortyx californicus*. Has a short, black plume curving forward from crown of head. Valley and foothill. 14, 40

QUAIL, MOUNTAIN, *Oreortyx pictus*. Long, straight head plume. Forest and brush in mountains. 48, 99

RABBIT, BRUSH, *Sylvilagus bachmani*. Weighs about half as much as cottontail rabbit. Chaparral from northern Oregon to southern Baja California. Rabbit young are born blind and almost hairless in a fur-lined nest. American rabbits don't live in burrows. 36

RACCOON, *Procyon lotor*. North Amer-

ica, except desert and boreal regions. Also introduced in Europe, Asia. Reasons why raccoons may "wash" food are still unclear. 21

RASPBERRY, *Rubus leucodermis*, Rose Family. Western raspberry. Berries black or red. Foothills and mountains to seven thousand feet. 68

RAT, NORWAY, *Rattus norvegicus*. Gray belly, scaly tail. Originally an Asian species. 28

RATTLESNAKE, *Crotalus viridis*. Western rattlesnake. Yellow, gray brown, or red body with brown or black blotches. Only poisonous snake in Yolla Bollys. 55

RAVEN, *Corvus corax*. Common raven. Distinguished from crow by larger size, wedge-shaped tail, heavier bill, and deeper voice. Rough country, deep forest. 48

RINGTAIL, *Bassariscus astutus*. Ringtailed cat, cacomixtle. May live in cabins or visit feeding stations, otherwise rarely seen. 108

ROBIN, *Turdus migratorius*. American robin. This large thrush breeds from Alaska to Texas, winters from Canada to Guatemala. 50, 71, 77, 99

ROTIFER, class Rotifera. Wheel animalcule. Microscopic but multicellular aquatic invertebrates. 79

ROUNDWORM, class Nematoda, Nematode. Microscopic or submicroscopic cylindrical worms, often incredibly abundant in soil or water. May be parasitic or free living. 79

RUSH, family Juncaceæ. Herbaceous monocots with cylindrical, often hollow stems. Mostly on wet ground. 53, 59, 75

SANDPIPER, SPOTTED, *Actitis macularia*. Teeter tail, tip up. Breast is only spotted during breeding season. Common shorebird along freshwater in most of Canada and United States. 79, 82, 100

SCORPION, genus *Vejovis*, order Scorpionida. Sting at end of tail is not dangerous to humans in northern California scorpions. 36

SEDGE, family Cyperaceæ. Herbaceous monocots with solid, often triangular stems and grasslike leaves arranged in threes. Wet or dry ground. 59, 75

SHOOTING STAR, genus *Dodecatheon*, Primrose Family. Blossoms with backward bending petals and forward pointing anthers, look like shooting stars. Pink, purple, or white. Leaves in a ground rosette. 76

SHREW, WANDERING, *Sorex vagrans*. Vagrant shrew. The common shrew of western mountains. Reddish brown to black. Small even for a shrew. 68

SILVERFISH, genus *Mesomachilis*, order Thysanura. Bristletail. The civilized silverfish of bathrooms and basements belong to a different family than this wilderness insect. 56

SKINK, *Eumeces skiltonianus*, western skink. A genus of medium-sized lizards which have bright blue stripes along their tails when young. Stripes fade on older individuals. 14

SKUNK, STRIPED, *Mephitis mephitis*. This member of the Weasel Family lives throughout the United States, southern Canada, and northern Mexico. 37, 65

SNAKE, GARTER, genus *Thamnophis*. Commonest snakes in North America, with many species. Maximum length four feet. Aquatic and terrestrial. Gray body with yellow stripes or light spots. Viviparous. 12

SNAKE, GOPHER, *Pituophis melanoleucus catenifer*. Bull snake. To five feet. Buff-colored body with brown or black, oval or square blotches. A curiously peaceful snake in my experience (having stumbled over it a number of times), but is said to hiss, bite, and rattle tail against dry leaves when cornered. 33

SPARROW, CHIPPING, *Spizella passerina*. White eye stripe and rusty cap. Throughout North America. 49

SPARROW, LINCOLN'S, *Melospiza lincolnii*. Gray-faced sparrow of wet places, mainly in West. 94, 98

SPIDER, COBWEB WEAVER, family Theridiidæ. A large family that spins irregularly shaped webs. Includes house spider, black widow. Most spiders can only be identified as to species by keying them out according to minute anatomical characteristics. 52

SPIDER, DWARF, subfamily Micryphantinæ. Over a million of these sequin-sized spiders may live in an acre of grassland. Little is known about them, except that they constantly eat insects and are more vulnerable to pesticides than insects because they breed more slowly. 80

SPIDER, DYSDERID, family Dysderidæ. Nocturnal spiders with six small eyes. 90

SPIDER, *Euryopis*, genus *Euryopis*, family Theridiidæ. 56

SPIDER, FILMY DOME, genus *Linyphia*, subfamily Linyphiinæ. Often abundant in pine forest. 66, 71

SPIDER, FUNNEL WEAVER, family Agelenidæ. On dewy mornings, grasslands are often seen to be full of this group's webs. 23, 60

SPIDER, *Geolycosa*, genus *Geolycosa*, family Lycosidæ. Digs burrows with jaws (cheliceræ). 60

SPIDER, JUMPING, family Salticidæ. Stout, droll, often brightly colored little spiders. The clowns of the arachnid world. 77

SPIDER, LONG-JAWED ORB WEAVER, genus *Tetragnatha*, family Araneidæ. Very elongated legs and bodies—like spiders reflected in a funhouse mirror. 50

SPIDER, ORB WEAVER, family Araneidæ. Large family that spin the classic circular, regular web. Spiderlings can spin perfect webs soon after hatching. 30, 53, 66, 80, 99

SPIDER, *Phidippus*, *Phidippus clarus*, family Salticidæ. A common, easily identified jumping spider with a black, red-striped, white-spotted body. Throughout North America. 48

SPIDER, SAC, family Clubionidæ. Nocturnal hunters that rest during the day in a flat, tubular sac beneath a log or stone. 80

SPIDER, SHEETWEB WEAVER, subfamily Linyphiinæ. Spiders of this group are often abundant. Filmy dome spiders are sheetweb weavers. 23

SPIDER, *Tidarren*, genus *Tidarren*, family Theridiidæ. 23

SPIDER, WOLF, genus *Lycosa*, family Lycosidæ. Large, common spiders, gray or brown. Often striped. Female carries a whitish egg sac until spiderlings hatch, at which time they ride around on her body for several days before scattering. If egg sac is taken away, female may substitute a snail shell or bit of bark. 23, 52, 60, 77, 78

SQUIRREL, DOUGLAS, *Tamiasciurus douglasii*. Chickaree, red squirrel. Mainly in lodgepole-fir forest but also in ponderosa. Small, dark brown squirrel with buff belly. 49, 65, 82, 91, 100

SQUIRREL, NORTHERN FLYING, *Glaucomys sabrinus*. Mixed conifer and hardwood forest through western mountains and Canada into Alaska. Prefer red fir and black oak in California. 58, 65, 90, 94, 110

STAR-THISTLE, YELLOW, *Centaurea solstitialis*, Sunflower Family. Several other alien weeds are in this genus. 13, 36

SWALLOW, VIOLET GREEN, *Tachycineta thalassina*. Glossy greenish purple back, white breast, white patches on sides of base of tail. The common square-tailed swallow in West. 13, 16, 77

TARWEED, genus *Madia* and genus *Hemizonia*, Sunflower Family. Sticky, pungent resins in leaves and stem give these common grassland forbs their name. 11, 14

TERMITE, genus *Zootermopsis*, order Isoptera. 56, 89

THRASHER, CALIFORNIA, *Toxostoma redivivum*. Sickle-billed relative of the mockingbird. Common in chaparral. 15, 40

THRUSH, HERMIT, *Hylocichla guttata*. A drab brown thrush with gray sides and reddish tail which it raises and slowly lowers every few seconds. Forages for insects on forest floor. North America's answer to the nightingale—everyone should have a chance to hear its song. See Eliot's *The Waste Land*, Section V, "What the Thunder Said." (Eliot uses an outdated specific name in his notes to the poem.) 77, 111

TITMOUSE, *Parus inornatus*, plain titmouse. Crested, gray relative of chickadee, with similar calls. 12

TOAD, WESTERN, *Bufo boreas*. A very warty species, color variable depending on surrounding soil—gray, black, brown, greenish. Sometimes patches of orange or yellow colors resembling lichens on warts. Belly light with black spots. Valley to pine forests. 36, 52, 63, 111

TOWHEE, RUFOUS-SIDED, *Pipilo erythrophthalmus*. A large Sparrow Family species with handsome white, black, and reddish plumage. Common in most of United States but hides in brush or undergrowth. 32, 40

TOYON, *Heteromeles arbutifolia*, Rose Family. Evergreen shrub with toothed leaves and red berries. Foothills and canyons. 12, 33

TROUT, RAINBOW, *Salmo gairdnerii*. Endemic to West Coast, now planted in streams worldwide. 2, 76, 77, 94, 96, 102

VIOLET, WHITE, *Viola blanda*, Violet Family. 59

VOLVOCINES, Genus *Volvox*. There appears to be some doubt as to the classification of these spherical, multicellular green organisms. Zoologists claim the genus as a protozoan; botanists claim it as an alga. Some biologists place it outside the Plant and Animal Kingdoms entirely, classifying it with bacteria, protozoans, and various algæ and fungi in a third Kingdom called the Protista. 79

VULTURE, TURKEY, *Cathartes aura*. Turkey buzzard. The red-headed, brown-plumaged vulture common in most of United States. Uncanny ability to locate dead animals is probably due to telescopic eyesight. 13, 15

WARBLER, AUDUBON'S, *Dendroica auduboni*. The exclusively American family of wood warblers has been termed "the butterflies of the bird world" because of diversely colorful species. 49, 100, 102

WATER BOATMAN, family Corixidæ.

Similar to backswimmers, but swim right side up and are not voraciously predacious. Feed on plants and minute animals gathered with scoop-shaped front legs. 13, 50

WATER STRIDER, family Gerridæ. Narrow-bodied, long-legged bugs which skate on water's surface film. Preys on small insects. 12, 50, 97, 102

WEASEL, *Mustela frenata*, long-tailed weasel. One of commoner predators but moves about so quickly one rarely gets more than a glimpse of it. 66, 83, 91

WHITETHORN, *Ceanothus cordulatus*, Buckthorn Family. Mountain whitethorn, snowbrush. 54, 76

WILLOW, genus *Salix*, Willow Family. Moist soil at all elevations. Dense thickets harbor many nesting birds. 12, 28, 55, 57, 63, 64, 98

WOLF, *Canis lupus*. There is no apparent reason for the historical absence of wolves from all but the northeast part of California. 3

WOODLOUSE, order Isopoda. Pill bug, sow bug. Armored, segmented crustaceans that feed on fungi and humus. 90

WOOD RAT, bushy-tailed, *Neotoma ci-*

nerea. Pack rat, trade rat. Larger than dusky-footed wood rat. Both species may abscond with shiny objects—coins, eyeglasses, etc.—leaving a nut or other object they were carrying "in trade." This species lives in rocky, alpine areas in most of West. 82, 98

WOOD RAT, dusky-footed, *Neotoma fuscipes*. Pack rat, trade rat. This lowland species persists in brushy canyons within some urban areas. Large, pyramidal, stick nests are easy to spot. California west of Sierra crest, and western Oregon. 26, 32, 34, 58, 82, 92, 110

WREN, *Thryomanes bewickii*, Bewick's wren. A long-tailed, light brown wren. Three other wrens—house, canyon, and rock—nest in foothills. Bewick's is most likely to nest in a hole in a streambank. 12

YARROW, *Achillea millefolium*, Sunflower Family. Flat-topped, white flower clusters. Feathery leaves. 55, 76

YERBA SANTA, *Eriodictyon californicum*, Phacelia Family. Sticky, shiny, lance-shaped leaves have been used as a cold remedy when brewed into tea. Funnel-shaped blue or lavender flowers. 15

The Dark Range

DESIGNED BY JAMES ROBERTSON
THE TEXT TYPE IS UNIVERSITY OF CALIFORNIA OLD STYLE
DESIGNED BY FREDERIC W. GOUDY AND SET BY
MONOTYPE AT MACKENZIE HARRIS CORP.
TITLES WERE HANDSET AT THE YOLLA BOLLY PRESS
IN UNIVERSITY OF CALIFORNIA OLD STYLE
LITHOGRAPHED AT PRINCETON POLYCHROME PRESS
BOUND AT A. HOROWITZ & SON BOOKBINDERS